You could call this book right-on-ta helpful, incisive, playful, entertaining doctor-ordered, but you will have to I'm too busy laughing!

Richard A. Swenson, M.D.
Author of *The Overload Syndrome*

Ours is a world of frenzied activity. From childhood to old age, we live in a constant rush of *doing*. In *Martha to the Max,* Debi Stack humorously convinces us that who we *are* in Christ counts infinitely more than all the works we *do*. Let this book change your life. If you read it seriously, it will!

Grace Ketterman, M.D.
Author of *The Complete Book of Baby and Child Care*

Debi Stack has struck a nerve and has shed needed light on the area of "perfectionism." I have to admit to being a Martha to the Max. However, this book has helped me see the need to not only mellow and moderate my expectations but has also motivated me to continue my pursuit of the "better" focus. This book is a compassionate, yet poignant exhortation to the "Marthas" in our lives.

Annie Chapman
Author, with Steve Chapman, of *Wednesday's Prayer*

For those who struggle with expecting perfection from themselves and others, this book offers some wonderful advice. Debi Stack is masterful with her insights into the famous Martha in the Bible, and with humor and knowledge, she gives us a more in-depth understanding of her. This book can bring back the joy that is often missing in the lives of those who strive to do everthing to the max, and in the doing, place great burdens on themselves and unrealistic expectations on others. It also provides understanding for those who live or work with a perfectionist. Debi is a good writer, but she is more than that. She writes with practical understanding and biblically based solutions.

Mary Whelchel
Author of *The Christian Working Woman* and
The Snooze-Alarm Syndrome

As a recovering Martha (not cured, just in remission) and the author of a book about perfectionism, I appreciate Debi's light-hearted yet powerful insights. She offers practical and life-changing wisdom so that we can find the balance we need. In her book, you'll find the meaning of the "one thing" Jesus refers to and you'll discover peace.

Kathy Collard Miller
Author of *Why Do I Put So Much Pressure on Myself?*

Debi is one of the most talented writers in today's market. *Martha to the Max* is witty and intelligent and fun, but the message does not get lost in the cleverness. Debi gives me hope that God has a special place in His heart for us overcommitted, underappreciated, stressed-out 21st-century moms.

Rhonda Wheeler Stock

Martha to the Max is a fun, fresh, and fast read full of insight for recovering perfectionists that is both practical and applicable while leading her to the "one thing that will never be taken away."

Marita Littauer
President CLASServices, Inc.
Speaker/Author
Personality Puzzle, Come As You Are,
You've Got What It Takes

What a delight! In the fast paced, dot com world in which I live and work, *Martha to the Max* provided me with the tools to delete some unnecessary programs (and files) still on my "heart" drive. I giggled, gulped, winced, and sighed relief as Debi led me to a better understanding of myself. While a perfectionist like myself doesn't often experience warm fuzzies—it seems like I experienced at least one on every page as Debi seemed to rewind and fast forward through my life journey—replaying for me many of the same Martha-inducing experiences I knew as a child, teen, young adult, and parent. While I just loved her engaging and witty style, perhaps the greatest gift Debi provides is the biblical and practical solutions for containing our Type A personalities. I WILL recommend this book to our readers—and giggle as I do so.

Jennifer and Philip Rothschild, Publishers
WomensMinistry.net
. . . your source for women's ministry news events, ideas, and speakers.

A classic "been there, don't do that" handbook, *Martha to the Max* illustrates with humor and sensitivity Debi Stack's rise from the ashes of burnout, while offering a cool drink of water to those still morphing into Marthahood.

> Cheryl Gochnauer,
> recovering perfectionist and author of
> *So You Want to Be a Stay-at-Home Mom*

For those of us who struggle with putting our "work" before our "worship"—I highly recommend *Martha to the Max.*

> Jan Brown,
> Interactive Producer, Christianity Online
> (Christianity Today, Inc.)
> Author of *Meet Me at the Well*

Martha to the Max is a must-read for today's busy Christian woman. With the scriptural insight of a careful Bible scholar, the graphic metaphors of an accomplished wordsmith and the passion of one who's walked in Martha's sandals, Debi Stack presents a solid antidote to the project-filled, control-oriented lifestyle of so many Christian women and men. I've studied Martha and preached about her for years, but I learned a lot from reading Debi's book. It's packed with potentially life-changing insights for the Marthas of the New Millennium.

> Don Hawkins,
> Cohost, Back to the Bible

You are in for an incredible treat. Any woman who has struggled with overcommitment, stress and perfectionism will find hilarity, help and especially hope in these pages. Readers will enjoy Debi's fast paced storytelling while they gain new tools for managing their maxed out lifestyles. I will be recommending this often in my counseling practice.

> Dr. Chuck Lynch
> Author of *I Should Forgive, But . . .*

Debi Stack, with her crowd-pleasing style that is funny and fast, conducts workshops on writing and goal-setting. She uses humor to address women who struggle with overcommitment, perfectionism, and stress. Debi has been an editor, teacher, and ghostwriter, and her humorous essays or features have appeared in magazines such as *Writer's Digest, Moody, Kansas City Family,* and *The Kansas City Star Magazine.* Debi, her husband Neal, and their children, Elizabeth and Andrew, live in Missouri.

MARTHA
to the
MAX

Balanced Living for Perfectionists

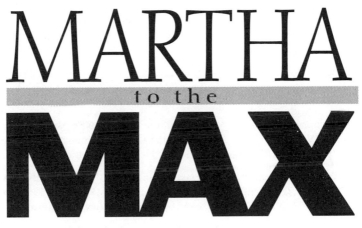

Debi Stack

MOODY PRESS
CHICAGO

All Scripture quotations, unless otherwise indicated, are taken from the *New King James Version*. Copyright © 1982 by Thomas Nelson, Inc. Used by permission. All rights reserved.

Scripture quotations marked NIV are taken from the *Holy Bible, New International Version*®. NIV®. Copyright © 1973, 1978, 1984 by International Bible Society. Used by permission of Zondervan Publishing House. All rights reserved.

Scripture quotations marked NASB are taken from the *NEW AMERICAN STANDARD BIBLE*®, © Copyright The Lockman Foundation 1960, 1962, 1963, 1968, 1971, 1972, 1973, 1975, 1977, 1995. Used by permission. (www.Lockman.org)

Scripture quotations marked TLB are taken from *The Living Bible* copyright © 1971. Used by permission of Tyndale House Publishers, Inc., Wheaton, Illinois 60189. All rights reserved.

Scripture quotations marked NLT are taken from the *Holy Bible, New Living Translation,* copyright © 1996. Used by permission of Tyndale House Publishers, Inc., Wheaton Illinois 60189, U.S.A. All rights reserved.

Scripture quotations marked *The Message* are from *The Message,* copyright © by Eugene H. Peterson 1993, 1994, 1995. Used by permission of NavPress Publishing Group.

Library of Congress Cataloging-in-Publication Data

Stack, Debi.
    Martha to the max : balanced living for perfectionists / by Debi Stack.
      p.cm.
    Includes bibliographical references.
    ISBN 0-8024-5389-9 (trade)
     1. Perfectionism (Personality trait)—Religious aspects—Christianity.
    2. Christian women—Religious life. I. Title.

BV4597.58.P47 S73 2000
248.8'43—dc21

00-041586

3 5 7 9 10 8 6 4 2

Printed in the United States of America

To my favorite person, my husband.
Without you, none of my writing dreams would have come true.
Without you, none of the laundry for the past year would have gotten done, either.
My little heart still tap-dances when you walk into the room.

Contents

Foreword

I started reading the manuscript for Martha to the Max a few minutes after I picked it up from the hotel desk. I read it while standing in airport check-in lines and riding in shuttle buses. No doubt people wondered what was in that coverless blue book that caused me to smile so much!

Debi Stack not only understands the pain of perfectionism experienced by the "Marthas" of the world, but she has captured the essence of the cure. A sure way to get a laugh in one of Taming the Paper Tiger training session is to quote something I read years ago: "A perfectionist is someone who takes great pains—and gives them to everyone else!"

Paper piles up in our lives because of our good intentions. We save every catalog to be sure we can get the best price or the perfect gift; keep more magazines than we could read in a lifetime because, after all, we must be knowledgeable; and agonize about what to do with all the artwork our children create, fearing we might damage them permanently if they see it in the trash! In fact, we are teaching them a lesson which many parents need desperately to learn: Life is a series of choices, and the quality of our life is directly related to our ability to let go of some very good things in order to ensure that we focus on what is best. Papers elicit perfectionism, because they represent our hopes, dreams, and intentions—and when papers remind us of our failure to live up to our own, frequently unrealistic, expectations, we feel and act like Martha!

The most frustrating aspect of being in the professional organizing business is that we are frequently confused with perfectionists. Clients are sometimes fearful that we might want to turn them into a "Martha"—when the real truth is that we want them to use organizing skills to help them become more like her sister Mary!

If you're overwhelmed by your own good intentions, be sure to read *Martha to the Max* to the very end. You'll not only understand why, but you'll be on the road to the peace of mind that all of us seek.

BARBARA HEMPHILL

Barbara Hemphill is CEO of Hemphill Productivity Institute, located in Raleigh, North Carolina, and author of the Taming the Paper Tiger series and *Simplify Your Workday*. She can be reached at www.productivityconsultants.com.

Acknowledgments

Underneath my name on the cover, it should say, "With a cast of thousands!" We'll fast-forward through most of those, such as "Second Teenaged Clerk at Kinko's" and "Microsoft Windows Support Technician at 3 A.M.," to see specific names deserving my gratitude.

Miss Steed and Mrs. Stafford, my grade school teacher and librarian, respectively, told me I had a gift for writing and never once laughed at the stories and poems I wrote. (To my face, anyway.)

Moody Press took a chance on me. What a super team! Special thanks, in order of appearance, go to Julie-Allyson Ieron, now of Joy Media, Inc.; Kelly Cluff; Jim Bell; Cheryl Dunlop; Linda Haskins; Anne Scherich; Dave DeWit; Carolyn McDaniel; and Ragont Designs.

Members of the Kansas City Christian Writers' Network understand what it's *really* like to write. Consider all two hundred of yourselves hugged!

A few names merit special mention: Charlotte Adelsperger, Mark Failing, Shawnee Fleenor, Cheryl Gochnauer (from whom I was separated at birth), Karen Hayse, Jeanette Littleton, Ellen Nelson, Dorothy Mock, Nancy Moser, Rhonda Stock, Sally Stuart, R. J. Thesman, and Teresa Vining. You were the difference-makers.

Mega-thanks to Mat Casner of Redlogic Communications for the awesome design of my web site, maxedout.net.

My friends at NHM, at MOPS, at LSCC, and everyone who received my prayer card (all 1,300 of you).

To the people who first suggested to me, nearly twenty years ago, that maybe, just maybe, people really are more important than projects.

To Roxie Ann Wessels, for affirmation.

To Charlene Osborn, my VP of E (vice-president of everything), who invested in me in every sense of the word. Viva la Tippins!

To Mom and Dad, thanks for always loving me, applauding whatever I did, and filling our home with good laughs and great books. Thanks for my new office. Thanks for helping with the kids while I wrote. I love you.

Mom Stack, you are the best mother-in-law in the world. Thanks for supporting my writing, giving me office supplies for Christmas (including my first computer—yea!), and for loving me like your own daughter. I love you.

Elizabeth, you are a princess! I could go around the world with you. Your help and understanding during this project inspired me. I love you.

Andrew, you are a prince! Thanks for regularly coming in my office to get lovies and to share your Twizzlers with me. I love you.

Most of all, thanks to God for using me in spite of myself. I love You.

I Was Sinking Deep in Sin (Whee!)

Every office has its Twilight Zone. The closet or stock area from which unwitting employees never return.

For me, it was the storage room at the ministry where I worked in the 1980s. A vast, untamed jungle of leaning shelves, twisted Venetian blinds, mildewed boxes, and reams of worthless records. Dust covered the new supplies, which covered the old supplies, which covered the chipped-tile floor from wall to wall.

Teresa, my co-worker, best friend, and a die-hard workaholic herself, took the initiative. We walked down the ministry's main hall to the last room on the left. (Isn't there a horror movie about such a location?) She turned on the light switch. One florescent bulb out of four flickered and hummed overhead, as if to say, "I can't hold on much longer!" Teresa swept the storeroom with a disdainful eye, then turned to me.

"This storage room is pathetic."

"Filthy."

"No one cares about this room. Everyone just crams stuff in here that really belongs in the trash."

"Disgusting."

"No one can find supplies when they need them, so they just order new ones. And the few important records the ministry needs can't be found because of all the junk piled on top of them. This room" (which she said in the "That dog!" tone pet owners use during the housebreaking stage) "is a source of stress and shame to everyone."

I brightened at a new thought. "And it's a fire hazard!"

Teresa brightened, too. "You're right. It's up to *us* to do something."

She didn't have to ask me twice. I'd been longing after that room with every color-coded gene in my body since I first opened its door.

At 7:00 A.M. one Saturday, we started cleansing the temple. We worked like fevered priests, purging the inner sanctum of disorganization and debris.

"Can you believe some of this stuff?" Teresa asked as she held up a bowling ball. "Why did anyone think this belonged in here?"

"Beats me," I muttered from under a sagging worktable where I'd found five cartons of shrink-wrapped letterhead—all with outdated addresses. "Some people don't have a clue about what to keep and what to throw away."

When we broke for lunch that afternoon at three o'clock, we didn't put our feet up and relax. While we ate yogurt and granola bars, we pored over office supply catalogs. The glossy pages of lateral file cabinets, storage bins, and label makers inspired us to transform the musty storage tomb into a well-lighted showcase of our organizational ability.

This project took more than one Saturday. We postponed hauling black trash bags of junk to the dumpsters until dark lest an observant pack rat try to stop us. Why did someone keep 582 leftover brochures from a fund-raiser in 1973? We kept 10 in a labeled folder, which went in the new box for the 1970–75 archives. Why did someone keep an office chair with three wheels and no back? We ordered an ergonomically smart new one on sale and got free shipping to boot.

At last, the day arrived to unveil this wonder to the other staff members. Their wide-eyed awe of the transformed room rewarded our efforts. Crisp-lettered signs hung everywhere, pointing out the obvious. Our guided tour of the new storage room had a condescending tone.

"See this bin with the label marked 'pens'? All the pens are in this bin."

The glory lasted for about a week. Teresa and I fumed and grieved over the shameless treatment of our crowning achievement.

"Why can't they put things back where they belong?"

"They don't see the obvious."

"Nothing gets done around here unless we do it ourselves."

"They don't care."

"Why do we even bother to make things nicer?"

We had a serious "us versus them" complex based not on color, sex, race, or religion but on personality type: A versus B.

TYPECASTING

Back in the 1980s, you could hardly pick up a magazine, tune in a radio station, watch a talk show, or read the *New York Times* best-seller list without finding at least one reference to the Type A personality. Describing the same personality type today, you might find buzzwords like *driven, perfectionist, workaholic, overachiever, tireless servant, superwoman, mover and shaker, power-hungry,* and *obsessive-compulsive.* (Since Marthas are always interested in saving time, let's call that last one "O-C" for short.) Most of these terms are self-explanatory, but O-C may be new to you. Here's a quick definition.

Individuals with this particular cluster of personality traits tend to be conscientious, self-sacrificing, organized, perfectionistic, and devout.[1]

Ooo! I like that! No wonder Teresa and I joined the "Type A, O-C, Martha-to-the-Max" union on the spot. Not only did we admire these qualities, we exemplified them beautifully in our storage room project.

Being conscientious and discerning (or uptight and judgmental, depending on your perspective), Teresa and I saw everything as perfect or putrid, right or wrong. So, because we were Type A's, we were right. That made everyone else a Type B, and it also made them (you guessed it) *wrong.* Simple, isn't it? Had we read this definition further, we might not have been so proud of ourselves since it calls perfectionism a "difficulty" and says Type A people are more prone to burnout, depression, and other not-so-good things. And all the while, Teresa and I thought perfectionism was a coveted personality trait bestowed upon a blessed few. Had we the power, we would have injected a dose of it into most other people we knew. So, while the terms may change to suit trends, the behavior —and its problems—is as timeless as ever.

AND NOW, BACK TO OUR PROGRAM

Of course Teresa and I were superior. As classic perfectionists, we easily spotted ways to improve everything. We planned ahead. We made lists. We designed charts. We skipped lunch. We worked overtime without pay. We proudly did the work of two or three people each. And we considered the Type B's surrounding us as our cross to bear on earth.

The Type B's didn't have a clue about time management. As classic social butterflies, organization to them was not a thing to *do* but a thing to *join* for the nifty membership pin and free refreshments. They viewed deadlines as suggested time frames to begin a project, not have it done. They actually sat around and talked during lunch. They left work promptly at 5:00 P.M. each afternoon. They drove us *nuts.*

Teresa and I piously comforted each other with the assurance that in heaven, there will not be "types" of people because we'll all be the same. Then she asked the question that began changing my life: "Are they going to be like us, or are we going to be like them?"

Whoa! Me? Demoted to be like them? It would be like having my wings clipped; being exiled to an alien planet; being a writer who's run out of similes.

Then a verse came to mind about what happens when we reach heaven: "We will be like Him."[2] That sounded to me as if all believers will be like Christ. But my ever-evaluating mind wanted to know who would have to change the most to be like Christ—the Type A's or the Type B's? Certainly if heaven is perfect and Christ is perfect, then perfectionistic Type A's would require little improvement compared to the lackadaisical Type B's.

Then another verse came to mind: "Pride goes before destruction."[3]

GOING RETRO

That scenario of perfectionistic behavior took place in the early 1980s, and I still can't decide whether to be proud or ashamed of it. Sure, I got a lot done and people commended me for my outstanding work ethic. But the short-lived glory was just a thin coating over a constant feeling of doom. Before me, I saw endless projects needing to be done. Behind me, I saw endless projects needing to be redone. And there I was in the middle—spinning my workaholic wheels as fast as I could, but not daring to stop and ask why.

Have you ever felt that way? Do you feel that way now? If so, you probably also fear, as I did, that life will *always* be this way. The light burden and easy yoke Jesus spoke of sounds wonderful—and completely unrealistic. After all, how can we rest when there is so much work to be done? And why in the round world don't the Type B people around us share our urgency to complete project after project?

We're not the first women to ask this question. First-century Bethany in Palestine boasted its own resident, Type A, workaholic woman. This powerhouse sister of Mary and Lazarus often opened her home to Jesus when He traveled near Jerusalem. Frustrated with shouldering all the happy hostess work herself (again), Martha asked Jesus why He didn't light a fire under her starry-eyed sister Mary so she'd help, too. His reply has been nagging me for years:

"Martha, Martha, . . . you are worried and upset about many things, but only one thing is needed. Mary has chosen what is better, and it will not be taken away from her."[4]

So what's wrong with Martha wanting to be a good hostess? I totally understand her wanting her environment to be ordered, her home to be spotless, and her projects to be flawless.

But such lofty expectations, I've since learned, often create a cycle of anger, frenzied work, and depression. Why don't the people around me notice what obviously needs to be done? Why don't they appreciate my self-sacrificing efforts to make things better? Why, no matter how hard I work, can I not achieve perfection, let alone maintain it?

If you've asked these same questions of yourself, consider this book a personal letter to you, written with the heartfelt love and hard-earned insight from me and other Christian women who've lived, and are still living, the struggle between naturally being like Martha and choosing to be like Mary.

Like Martha, I am tempted to perfect my own personal kingdom, not seek the kingdom of God. Like Martha, I tend to view life as a series of projects, not a path toward knowing and serving Christ.

And yet, the inherent perfectionistic Martha-qualities are there by God's design.

Eric Liddell, the 1930s Olympic runner profiled in the award-winning movie *Chariots of Fire,* said, "The Lord made me fast, and when I run I feel His pleasure." The challenge for Marthas today regarding their abilities is to view them and use them in a way that brings a smile to the face of God.

ROAD WORRIER

There's one in every family.

This is the person who gets the most mileage out of travel plans by obsessing over uncontrollable details way in advance— fuel prices, traffic flow, the weather. "Sorry kids, but I'm canceling the road trip to Yosemite. There's a cloud in the sky somewhere over Nebraska. It's just not worth the risk."

Departing from a maxed-out lifestyle toward unknown territory may raise some worries in your mind, too. While it may *feel* safer to stay on familiar home ground, doing so means missing out on all kinds of wonderful stuff. Breathtaking vistas. Heart-stopping natural wonders. A set of toothpick holders imprinted with "DELBERT'S TRUCK STOP."

Besides stocking up on antacids, plan to encounter lots of detours, delays, and orange barrels. Why? Because far from being a straight and smooth superhighway, the path toward discovering the "one thing" that Jesus told Martha was needed is a bumpy, meandering road under construction. Though I looked long and hard for a shortcut to the "one thing," none could be found. Along the way, though, I discovered things about myself, my perceptions, my relationships, and my health that I'll share with you. They include:

— insight into how we get ourselves so maxed out
— the similarities between Martha of Bethany and us
— the surprising source of perfectionism
— a predictable pattern to overworking and burnout (plus how to overcome it!)
— how to relax even when we're not in the mood and don't have time
— freedom from the maxed-out lifestyle
— and more!

So read on. Watch me go over the bumps, miss my exit, and run out of gas. Eventually, I find what I believe to be the "one thing" Jesus spoke of. When you find it, too, I think you'll agree that all those orange barrels are worth their weight in gold.

CHAPTER TWO

Testing, Testing ... How Much of a Martha Are You?

Hold it right there.

If you're one of those types of people who think there aren't any types of people, you probably never went to camp as a kid.

At camp, where attendees are supposed to become one peaceful tribe, warring bands form shortly after arrival. Kids who have never seen each other before mysteriously break into types and gravitate together. The renegade girls who sneak in with cigarettes and out with boys somehow find each other. The brainy boys who handle snakes and compasses with equal ease, if not equal skill, find each other too. ("Sheldon! Quick! Before you pass out, which way is north and how do we make a tourniquet?")

Even if the kids didn't naturally group together, their counselors would do it for them. Imagine what would happen at a Bible camp with a Twenty-third Psalm theme. A camp leader tweets her whistle and gives orders on which kids go to which cabins.

"All first-timers who've never even spent the night at your grandma's house and are trying really hard not to cry, line up and follow your counselor to the Valley of the Shadow of Death.

"Bed wetters, follow your counselor to My Cup Runneth Over.

"Campers who, against policy, have smuggled banned items of any kind, including tobacco and electronics, will bunk with me, the camp director, and her pit bull in The Presence of My Enemies."

What's that you say? You never went to camp? Certainly you've watched television!

TV scriptwriters have long used personality conflict as the basis of both drama and comedy. Remember the Clampetts from *The Beverly Hillbillies?* Their backwoods upbringing was comical because it was plopped into a refined and elegant setting. And don't forget the Douglases from *Green Acres.* Their cultured New York background made their new life in Hooterville a real hoot. Leaving those fictional families in their original settings, surrounded by others who thought and acted exactly as they did, wouldn't have been even a fraction as funny.

Watching these characters interact (and in some cases, overact) is entertaining. But living the same kind of personality conflict in the real world is not. If you're a project-oriented Type A Martha who's ever butted heads with a people-oriented Type B Mary, you know exactly what I'm talking about. It's awful. It's irritating. It's like chewing foil. But it's not incurable! As we move together through this book, we'll learn how to minimize the stressful "us versus them" attitude.

But for now, since I have systematically proven from backbreaking, in-depth research that yes, indeed, there *are* definite types of people in the world, I deserve to take a short break. The only question remaining is, should I watch *Gilligan's Island* or *I Dream of Jeannie?**

* You'll notice throughout this book that all my television references are to shows from the 1960s and 1970s. This is because I am the sum total of my viewing experiences, and that's when most of them happened. Plus, the shows nowadays are all about hip singles full of angst, innuendo, and tofu. I just can't relate.

I CAN TYPE 75 PEOPLE A MINUTE

Grouchy as a bear. Meek as a mouse. Strong as an ox. Cold as a fish.

Distant. Emotional. Workaholic. Bum.

Introvert. Extrovert.

Type A. Type B.

We ever-evaluating Marthas size up others everywhere we go and slap labels on them before you can say "self-righteous." I've always done this while priding myself that I'm not like all those *other* Christians who use personality type as sanctified horoscopes to pigeonhole, prophesy, and pass judgment.

"He obviously lacks motivation."

"Their marriage won't last. Everyone knows their temperaments don't mix."

"She overeats because she's introverted."

"Type A's are better than Type B's because they get the job done, and done right the first time." (Well, that one's true, isn't it?)

You know from reading so far that I consider myself a Type A, Martha person. Probably you consider yourself to be a Martha, too. There are literally hundreds of personality and temperament tests available, and I could have used one of those in this book, but why take the easy way out? True to my Martha nature of doing and redoing everything myself, I made my own test.

Please remember that the test below, and, yea, verily, this whole book, is written for Christian women who are maxed out with perfectionism and can't remember the last time they had a good laugh at themselves. This book is not intended for readers who are so consumed by perfectionism or obsessive-compulsive behavior that simple daily functions are continually disturbed.[1] If you have crossed the line between these two, please seek help from a qualified professional. The resources today are wonderful and plentiful! Even better, the love, mercy, and healing grace of God are available to you in unlimited measure. A list of starting places is in chapter 18, "Resources".

THIS IS ONLY A TEST

Before we get started, let's review the three schools of Type A thought about taking tests in books, magazines, and other printed material.

Emblazon Academy: This school condones use of a four-color pen or a variety of highlighters to mark up the pages like graffiti on a warehouse. This will flaunt your mastery of the material to the next reader, who probably needs all the help she can get.

The Institute of Immaculate Examinations: This school leaves each pristine page unsullied by ink of any sort. An occasional faint pencil mark in the margin is acceptable, but these must be completely erased lest the next reader sees your answers (which might be less than perfect, and we can't have that now, can we?).

Paranoia University: This school writes the answers on a separate sheet of paper and then shreds it, thus ensuring that the next reader can neither copy nor divulge your answers.

Now that you have your testing tools in hand, here's how to respond to the test.

This analysis is made up of a long list of statements concerning perfectionistic, O-C, Type A, Martha behavior. There are two possible responses to each statement: *True* or *False.*

> *Example:* I polish the light bulbs as part of my weekly housecleaning routine.

Perhaps you can honestly answer true. More likely, you're thinking, "Polish my light bulbs? Does *she* polish *her* light bulbs? Why didn't I think of that before? How can I live another day, another minute, with bacteria-laden layers of light bulb dust spawning disease in my home? My children probably have lungs like coal miners. I'm going to stop reading right now and polish every light bulb in my house, including the twenty-eight strings of miniature lights stored in the Christmas boxes."

WAIT! The light bulb thing was just an example. How about if I give you three possible responses instead of just two? *True, False,* and *False, but I ought to, need to, should be able to answer true, and I feel really, really guilty that I can't.*

Ready? Let's go!

1. I enjoy making lists.
2. I enjoy answering questions on a list.
3. A perfect day, to me, is accomplishing everything on a list.
4. People are the main obstacle between me and my list. (Are you beginning to see a pattern here?)
5. I will sometimes peek at the scoring system on quizzes to help me score higher. (By the way, it starts on page 25.)
6. Listening to people talk is usually a boring waste of time.
7. The recipe cards in my kitchen are alphabetized in protective plastic sleeves.
8. I have little tolerance for slow movers and slow thinkers.
9. Hardly anything moves me to tears, and I think people who cry easily are weak.
10. Unlike most of the people around me, I can perform several tasks simultaneously.
11. Bringing order out of chaos is one of my biggest thrills.
12. Catalogs and periodicals in my magazine rack at home are arranged chronologically.
13. People who use book bags instead of briefcases are inferior.
14. The spices in my kitchen are alphabetized.
15. I frequently get sidetracked from the main task at hand.
16. My personal devotions have a routine (when I have time to do them, that is).
17. Organizational skills are superior to relational skills.
18. People frequently compliment me on my organizational skills.
19. I do not understand why people feel hurt when I make an obvious and practical suggestion for improvement in their lives.
20. People rarely come to me with personal concerns. (Hmm . . . could there be a pattern here, too?)
21. Being sick, even for a day, makes me feel angry because it wastes time.
22. When I travel or eat alone, I always take something to read or work on.

23. I feel guilty if I sleep in (or sometimes for sleeping at all).
24. I do some of my best cleaning and organizing when I am angry.
25. I am early or right on time for appointments; if I'm late, it's never my fault.
26. Storage containers and closet systems are some of my favorite and most frequent purchases.
27. People who relax too much will regret it someday.
28. I can find a way to improve just about everything.
29. My grocery lists are made according to the floor plan of the supermarket.
30. I exercise good control over my finances and plan ahead for major expenses.
31. I don't enjoy holidays very much and am glad when they are over.
32. My office or work area is neat and organized, but my home is often messy and cluttered (or vice versa).
33. I get a buzz out of seeing overtime hours on my paycheck.
34. I would find it easier to forgive people if they would just learn from their mistakes.
35. If I have to explain why a team goal was not met, I will not cover for the person who was at fault (and probably shouldn't have been on my team in the first place).
36. I am always aware of time and refer to my watch and daily planner frequently.
37. I have already made funeral plans.
38. The rush I get from finishing a major project, even if I stayed up all night to do it, compensates for the abuse my body took to get it done.
39. I report problems to managers at restaurants, hotels, stores, and other service places.
40. Family photos are all identified and organized in archival-quality systems.
41. I work harder than most people I know, yet there is no end to what needs to be done.
42. People who take breaks at work, including lunch breaks, have a lazy streak.
43. I enjoy talking about my goals and my progress toward them.

44. When someone tells me about a bad experience, I tell him about my similar (or worse) experience to help him feel better.
45. Frequently called telephone numbers are posted near each phone in a card system or typed list in a protective plastic sleeve.
46. When I pray, it is usually to ask for God's help in accomplishing my goals.
47. Plastic bags from the grocery store are folded in a neat pile.
48. I am bothered when other people believe they have to have the last word.
49. I hate lists that end unevenly.

Preliminary Scoring

Give yourself one point for every *True* or *Ought to* answer to the above 49 statements.

0–9 You're probably a classic Type B Mary (remember Martha's sister?) who wants either to hug me or shoot me. Both prospects are equally appalling. Instead, call a friend right now for a nice, long chat and use this book to press flowers.

10–29 Tell your friend you'll have to call her back because you're taking a test right now.

30–47 You're on the brink, teetering dangerously close to the Type B dark side. Quick! Reorganize a drawer, your purse—anything—and save yourself before it's too late! And may the list be with you.

48 Too bad, so sad. You were *so* close to having a perfect score.

49 Primo perfectionist! See if you can bag more points below.

Secondary Scoring

Add 500 bonus points if you skipped to this section before taking the test so as to boost your score.

Deduct 10,000 points if you skipped to this section and had no intention of taking the test.

Add 25,000 bonus points if you took the whole test in one sitting.

Deduct 5,000,000 points if you started the test but quit before finishing.

Grand Total Scoring

-5,010,000 to 25,548	Thanks for playing along and enjoy this lovely parting gift—a glow-in-the-dark ceramic replica of *The Thinker* wearing a festive ball-fringed sombrero.
25,549	Congratulations! You're in the gloating company of many other world-class, die-hard, Type A, Marthas-to-the-Max.

DISHING IT OUT

Most of the time, we Marthas like things that fall into two neat categories. A razor-sharp dividing line separates the right and the wrong, the *either* and the *or,* the black and the white. Decisions are a snap. There's no agonizing over multiple solutions that could all be equally valid (as if!). Not only does rushing to judgment save time, it's the only form of exercise we get on most days.

There are times, though, when this all-or-nothing mind-set hits too close to home.

According to the above test, you're either a Martha to the Max or you're not. Anything less than 25,549 on the screwball scoring system, and you'll never learn the secret handshake.* Actually, you, me, and any other woman can be a Martha because Marthaness doesn't depend on our list's length, but on its weight. It's not how many demands we have in our lives, but how we perceive them and our ability to meet them. I'm convinced that if I did an "Are you maxed out?" survey on any street, almost every woman would answer with a resounding yes. Perhaps she's only working on three

---

* It's not a handshake at all, but a pointing index finger used to punctuate phrases like, "That doesn't belong there," "You were supposed to have cleaned that up an hour ago," and "I'll tell you what your problem is!"

things. Or thirty-three. Either way, if she feels closer to the end of her rope than the end of her list, she's maxed out.

There are those few mutant women out there who can have jam-packed personal planners and somehow sail through each day and sleep through each night. Marthas do neither. We're too uptight, stressed out, and overcommitted. The good news is that while our problems are common, they're not incurable. We have hope! Living every minute of every day on the verge of spontaneous combustion will soon be a thing of the past. The good things we'll replace it with will never be taken from us.

Before we go one step further, we've got to take several steps back—back to an ancient village called Bethany. Yes, it's a rustic area, but if you have any camping experience at all, you'll do fine. One more thing—unless you like pit bulls, don't smuggle any contraband.

CHAPTER THREE

Martha's World: It Never Stops Spinning

Say the name *Martha* today, and most people will think of tasteful-living guru Martha Stewart. What would *she* suggest we pack as we travel to ancient Bethany? Maybe something like this.

"The secret to dressing for distant and warmer climes is cotton. Lots and lots of cotton. My favorites comprise this mix-and-match ensemble of thirty-seven garments. I sewed these myself, from fabric I wove myself, from cotton I grew myself. You can do the same. It's really quite simple. These outfits are perfect for any Middle Eastern country from which Americans have not yet been forcibly evacuated."

War has been a fact of daily life in this region for thousands of years. Can it further withstand a volley of Stewartesque comments?

I think not.

Let's just pretend we're already packed to perfection. Even our passport photos look good! Our immunizations are up-to-date, our planes are on time, and delightful little chocolates are on the nightstand in our air-conditioned hotel rooms. Before we set out, though, let's scope out the area and gather clues that will all come together in the next chapter.

★   ★   ★

In size, ancient Palestine was comparable to New Jersey.[1]

In climate, it was much like southern California.[2]

Its population was about 250,000 nationwide, roughly the same as Las Vegas today.[3]

Our main interest, Bethany, lies about two miles southeast of Jerusalem. Today, its ruins lie within a poor Arab[4] village with a population of about 3,500.[5] Its name is now El Azaryiah for its most famous citizen—the resurrected Lazarus.[6] His supposed tomb, a cave really,[7] is open to tourists who care to descend dozens of steep, rock-hewn steps to the burial chamber.[8] But he's not our focus on this trip. His sister Martha *is.*

BEAUTIFUL DOWNTOWN BETHANY

This village's name means "house of dates"[9] because lovely palm trees were one of its outstanding features. One account says ancient Bethany was "remarkably beautiful, the perfection of retirement and repose, of seclusion and lovely peace."[10] Today, most of bygone Palestine's natural forests are depleted,[11] making it even in Jesus' time "comparatively desolate, barren, grey."[12] This may account for other sources saying Bethany also means "house of misery"[13] or "house of poverty."[14]

Situated about two miles from Jerusalem on the southeastern slope of the Mount of Olives, Bethany was the last major town on the road to Jericho.[15] When this land belonged to the Israelite tribe of Benjamin, it was called Beit Hanania.[16] Primarily an agricultural area, its people produced grapes, apricots, melons, pomegranates, figs, dates, olives, wheat, barley, spelt, beans, lentils, and wine in addition to pasturing sheep and goats.[17] (Strangely, there is no mention of cotton.) An excavation in the early 1950s unearthed cisterns, houses, winepresses, and silos[18]—signs of an active village.

Jesus' visit there, as recorded in Luke 10:38–42, took place in the year A.D. 29 between the Feast of Tabernacles (Jewish month of Tishri in our September–October[19]) and the Feast of Dedication (Jewish month of Chislev in our November–December[20]).[21] This means He arrived at the beginning of Palestine's rainy season.[22] Exactly the time of year any hostess would love to have company. No sunny weather with which to air your best linens or shake your dusty rugs. Trouble finding dry fuel for the fire. Sheep, goats, and chickens all making noise and trying to nudge their way under your sheltering roof. Children underfoot. Yep. The ideal time to put one in the mood for graceful entertaining.

If the house of Martha, Mary, and Lazarus were a simple Palestinian home, it was probably made of native limestone to withstand the seasonal torrential rains, had a flat roof, measured about fifteen feet by fifteen feet, and had an oven outside under a shelter.[23] If they were very poor, their meals would be served on a mat of some kind placed on the floor.[24]

If their house were what we'd call middle-class, it would have at least double the square footage to allow for stabling livestock, separate rooms for men and women, and possibly even a second floor.[25] As for furniture, they might have "a table, a few chairs or stools and benches, sometimes beds and chests. People usually slept on the floor or on stone or brick benches attached to the walls and covered with mats or animal skins."[26] Common dishes were made from easily broken ceramic. Jugs and other containers might have small holes around the rim through which twine or wire could be threaded to form a handle. Palestinian ceramics were not glazed, but some were painted brown or red.[27]

If these siblings were wealthy, their dwelling would be more of a compound than a house. Built around a central courtyard,[28] their many-roomed home might even be made of costly cedar imported from Lebanon.[29] Other materials—such as ivory, stone, and metals —might be used, too.[30] The roof over the rich was likely to be inclined and covered with tiles.[31] Instead of a ladder, as moderate homes had, a staircase would lead to the upper level.[32] A finely appointed guest room would be built near the main entrance.[33] Guests' supper in the evening was served in a room lit nearly as bright as day with many oil lamps[34] and filled with music.[35]

A central kitchen might be found,[36] and the shelves might display fine Tiberian glassware—the thinnest and most beautiful anywhere.[37] Add inside baths, frescoes on the plastered walls,[38] dining couches patterned after the Romans',[39] comfy beds patterned after the Egyptians',[40] and we're talking about a party worthy of a photo shoot for *House Beautiful*.

Which house was Martha's? My guess is the last. The Gospelwriter Luke ascribes authority, if not ownership, of the house to her, even though women there seldom inherited property. If her parents were dead, maybe she was acting as guardian until Lazarus would be old enough to assume the leadership role. She'd also require funds and space to properly host Jesus and all those who traveled with Him—no small feat because the cost of living in Judea was five times higher than in Galilee.[41] Plus, it was expected in small villages that only "an established household" would also be the first to extend hospitality.[42] Finally, Martha is remembered as being distracted with endless details. How many opportunities for detail-obsession do you think a one-room dwelling can offer? Not many compared to a spacious compound with every well-furnished room needing to be tweaked to perfection.

PRIDE AND PREJUDICE

Remember the stories about Jesus in Galilee? That was a region, not a city, in the northern part of ancient Palestine. Capernaum, Cana, and Nazareth are Galilean cities whose names are familiar to us because of the miracles Jesus performed there.

Now, imagine a small balloon attached to a very long string. Fastened at the end of the string is a pillowcase. The small balloon is the Sea of Galilee, the string is about sixty-five miles of the Jordan River, and the pillowcase is the Dead Sea. Less than ten miles directly west from where the end of the string ties onto the pillowcase is Jerusalem and Bethany. They are in the region known as

Judea.[43] Conclusion: Galilee is in the north, Judea is in the south, and they're connected by the Jordan River.

You know how in America there are certain stereotypes about southerners and northerners? Ancient Palestine had the same kind of regional racism. The people of each area were just as different as their terrains.

Galilee had an estimated "240 small towns and villages, each with not less than 15,000 inhabitants."[44] The landscape was "gloriously grand, free, fresh, and bracing. A more beautiful country, hill, dale, and lake, could scarce be imagined than Galilee Proper. . . . Proverbially, all fruit grew in perfection."[45]

Galileans were almost what today we'd call freethinking party animals. Regarding canon law, they "took independent views."[46] They were also "of generous spirit, of warm, impulsive hearts, of intense nationalism, of simple manners" as well as "excitable, passionate, violent."[47]

Did I mention that the apostle Peter was from Galilee?

Compared to flourishing, green Galilee, Judea is described as having "decaying cities of ancient renown; the lone highland scenery; the bare, rugged hills; . . . with distant glorious Jerusalem ever in the far background."

Judeans prided themselves on being cultured, studious, and pious.

> Greater contrast could scarcely be imagined than between the intricate scholastic studies of the Judeans, and the active pursuits that engaged men in Galilee. It was a common saying, "If a person wishes to be rich, let him go north; if he wants to be wise, let him come south." . . . There was a general contempt in Rabbinic circles for all that was Galilean.[48]

Jesus was born in Bethlehem—making Him Judean by birth. But because Jesus spent most of His adult life in Galilee, this likely fueled contempt for Him by Jerusalem's already-biased religious leaders.

THE UNBREAKABLE CODE

Generous hospitality is a time-honored hallmark of Middle

Eastern culture. The nomadic segment required temporary dependence upon locals for water, food, and shelter.[49]

Ancient Palestinians ate two meals a day—lunch at midday and supper in the evening.[50] Usually guests were invited to supper; only the wealthy entertained at breakfast.[51] For others, breakfast was such a small snack that it didn't merit even being called a meal.[52] As for food, half of their diet was grains; the other half was wine, oil, legumes, fruits, vegetables, and cheese.[53] The wealthy ate meat regularly, but the occasion of entertaining guests required meat no matter the host's station.[54]

Typically, visiting strangers/guests would wait in an obvious place, such as a city gate or well, to be noticed.[55] "The failure of a community to approach the strangers and issue an invitation before nightfall to dine and lodge in an established household was a serious breach of honor signifying an insult toward the strangers and an indication of the locals' bad character."[56]

For the people of God within that culture, hospitality attained even greater meaning. The Jewish faith began with a man on a journey—Abraham. Throughout the history of Judaism is story after story of wandering and homelessness. Inviting strangers into one's home—to feed, refresh, and protect them—is a picture of God's hospitality to Israel and ultimately to all the world. Hence, His command, "Therefore love the stranger, for you were strangers in the land of Egypt."[57]

Jesus further sanctioned unconditional hospitality when He said, "For I was hungry and you gave me something to eat, I was thirsty and you gave me something to drink, I was a stranger and you invited me in." When Jesus dispatched His disciples on their first solo ministry tours, He told them to depend on local hospitality. Any town that did not extend such was doomed.[58] (It's possible that the first personal contact Martha had with Jesus' disciples was when He sent the seventy out and she provided hospitality for some of them.)

A good host, which could be a man or a wealthy woman,[59] willingly offered nothing short of the very best for the guests.[60] Then followed a standard welcoming program.

When a guest arrives, the usual salutation given by the host, if both are of social equality, is a kiss. This salutation is first offered by the host and then returned by the guest. A slave is then summoned, girded with a towel around his waist and bearing a basin and [pitcher]. The former is placed underneath the bared hands and feet respectively, and the water from the [pitcher] is poured over them. A second slave also attends with the perfume which is sprinkled over the guest, and, in a rich house, a third slave may bring in a burning censer and a napkin with which the head is covered for a moment, so that the fragrant smoke of the incense may impregnate the garments of the guest. More rarely, costly essential oils or essences, such as attar of roses, may be dropped upon the head.

As the guests enter, if there be more than one, he who is highest in rank is placed on the right hand of the host. . . . For the left hand of the host is the second place of honor, the second on the right is the next place of honor, and so on alternately. . . . The lowest seat at the feast is the extreme left. This matter of position is very important in the Eastern code, and if a host finds that any of his guests are incorrectly placed, it is his duty to request that the matter be put right.

When the meal is ordered, the same command is used as in the days of the Old Testament: "Set on bread." Thereafter the slaves stand with their arms folded and their eyes intent upon those of the master of the house awaiting any fresh orders.

The food is placed in a common dish into which all dip their bread. . . . Water is not put on the table at meal times, but, like wine, is brought to those who call for it. The drinking cup is a small bowl without handles, usually of brass, and held from below, poised on the tips of the fingers. Like the dish, it is common to all who sit down.

After every meal an Oriental not only washes his hands, but also rinses his mouth with water.[61]

Guests could expect to stay two nights, unless the host urged a longer visit.[62] After this, the host would be required to send them off well supplied for their trip. "The goal at this final phase of hospitality was to have the guest depart in peace without having disrupted the social harmony of the household or the community."[63]

It seems that, when it comes to hospitality, peace is as important as honor.

A WOMAN'S PLACE

Into this physical setting, Martha shone like a diamond—but still in the coal stage. Living in a culture sharply divided along gender lines,[64] she had only two ways of excelling in her world: having sons[65] or being an exceptional hostess. Scripture doesn't mention Martha's being married so, for the time period in her life we're focusing on, that nixed the baby business. Hospitality, then, would receive her best efforts.

Martha would likely have known Jewish stories of those who extended great hospitality and were, in turn, richly rewarded by God Himself. Sarah and the Shunammite woman had baby boys. Abigail married King David. The widow at Zarephath never ran out of oil or flour. Rahab's family was spared in a battle.[66] We then see why Martha was so motivated to be an exceptional hostess to every guest under her roof: to protect the family honor, keep local gossips at bay, and perhaps—dare she hope?—gain a husband and children!

The place of Jewish women in ancient Palestine was below that of men as far as social freedoms. They were valued most for being pure before marriage and fertile after marriage.[67] Jesus' treatment of women, then, was amazing. Imagine a man being deeply interested in how a woman thinks and feels; not being ashamed to speak with her in public or to touch her for healing.[68] Strong-minded Martha must have looked on approvingly and thought, *It's about time!*

THE HONORABLE MS. MARTHA

There's one thing that I must emphasize about this culture because it bears so strongly on Martha's words and actions in the next chapter. Middle Eastern people prized one thing above all else: honor. This core value made them conflict-prone. Here's how researcher John Pilch explains it:

> Every person is presumed to be honorable and spends a lifetime guarding, protecting, and maintaining that honor. The ongoing cul-

tural "game" concerned with honor consists of "challenge and response." Individuals challenge the honor of their equals in hopes of shaming them (catching them off guard, unable to make an appropriate response), and thereby increasing their own honor. Such persons are truly "catalytic"; they enjoy lighting fires.[69]

The problem with igniting a confrontation over honor, though, is that someone always gets burned.

CHAPTER FOUR

The Strife of the Party

With that *"You . . . are . . . th–th–there!"* chapter behind us, all we need to do is review the cornerstone text, Luke 10:38–42. Then we'll be set to journey to another time and place . . . and meet someone we feel we've known all our lives.

> Now it happened as they went that [Jesus] entered a certain village; and a certain woman named Martha welcomed Him into her house. And she had a sister called Mary, who also sat at Jesus' feet and heard His word. But Martha was distracted with much serving, and she approached Him and said, "Lord, do You not care that my sister has left me to serve alone? Therefore tell her to help me." And Jesus answered and said to her, "Martha, Martha, you are worried and troubled about many things. But one thing is needed, and Mary has chosen that good part, which will not be taken away from her."

GUESS WHO'S COMING TO DINNER?

Surprises don't go over well with control-happy women. Was the original Martha one of them? We don't know for sure if Jesus' visit was prearranged or spontaneous. At the least, she might have had half-an-hour's notice. That's the time it took to walk from the Damascus Gate in Jerusalem to the village of Bethany.[1] Did young Lazarus run home to shout, "I got Him! He's coming!"

"Who's coming?" Martha asked, continuing to knead dough without looking up.

"Jesus!"

That got her attention. "*What!* When?"

"Now! He's on His way."

Lazarus might as well have blown a trumpet in the ear of a racehorse. From that moment on, Martha was a frenzied blur of activity. Even if her home was always tidy, there was plenty to do in preparation for guests. Not only did she need to arrange a sumptuous meal, but also be prepared to extend overnight hospitality.

How did she know who Jesus was? Martha would certainly have heard of, if not witnessed, Jesus' cleansing of the temple in Jerusalem two years before. (No jokes, please, about her pointing out, "You missed a spot.") Reports of His many miracles in Galilee likely trickled south to Judea—accounts of healing, feeding multitudes, and even walking on water!

Last year in Jerusalem, Jesus had healed a lame man. And this year in Jerusalem again, He healed the man born blind. Did Martha or her siblings witness any of the Jerusalem miracles firsthand? We don't know, but it's likely that, at the least, someone in their village did, who then reported the news to everyone.

Jesus seldom, if ever, traveled alone. All twelve disciples had been selected by this time. Knowing some of Jesus' followers were rough Galileans, Martha may have wanted to spare no expense and thus display refined Judean hospitality at its best (secretly hoping some of her cultured manners would rub off on them). It's known that women traveled with Jesus. Possibly a few Pharisees and Sadducees accompanied Jesus' group, either from curiosity or meanness. Martha's making a good impression on them wouldn't hurt Lazarus's future prospects any. At the least, Martha could expect half a dozen men. At the most, a group of men *and* women numbering perhaps fifty![2]

NO ONE'S IN THE KITCHEN WITH MARTHA

Being wealthy (as we are supposing here), Martha probably had a domestic staff.

Being *herself*, Martha probably had exacting standards that caused a high turnover rate. Imagine the placement coordinator of a temporary employment agency in Jerusalem reviewing a servant's résumé: "So you worked for Martha of Bethany. Who hasn't?"

And now, at the highest point of her hospitality career, just when she needed *everyone* to do her assigned duties without fail, her sister disappears. A young servant girl, whom we'll call Lydia, inched up to Martha, who rushed from one task to the other without actually finishing any of them.

"I . . . I . . . I'm sorry to interrupt, but . . . but . . . but . . ."

Martha wheeled around, hands on hips. "But *what!*"

". . . but we can't find the new brass platter."

"Ask Mary. She knows where it is." Martha turned her back and began fussing over goat cheese.

"I can't."

"Why ever not?"

"She's gone."

Martha wheeled around again, hands on Lydia. *"What do you mean she's gone?"*

"No one knows where she is."

In the blink of an eye, Martha stalked off—searching for her sister, irritation swelling inside of her with each step. On her way past the dining area, Martha did a double take. Jesus and Lazarus were seated in chairs at the highest table, their backs to her. When Jesus leaned slightly to the right, Martha thought she saw a flash of deep blue, the exact shade of Mary's head covering, in front of Jesus' place at the table.

No, it's gone.

There it is again!

Martha edged to the left . . . yes! It *is* Mary's head covering. What is she doing on the floor? Clumsy girl probably dropped something as she served. Why doesn't she hurry and get it picked up? There are a thousand other things to do.

Jesus leaned far to the right . . . and Martha saw Mary looking up at Jesus in rapt attention. She wasn't working. She was *sitting!*

★ ★ ★

Our English Bibles say simply, "Mary sat." That's not nearly as revealing as the original term used here. Out of thirteen possible Greek words meaning "sat," the Gospel-writer Luke could have used *kathemai*. It's the most-used term for the natural posture of sitting. But Mary wasn't merely sitting. He could've used *kataklino*. It's only used to mean sitting at a meal. But Mary wasn't sitting merely to feed her body. Luke used *parakathizo*,[3] a word that's never, ever used again in the entire New Testament because Mary sat in a way that no one else did: She sat very near. Mary sat to feed her soul.

BOILING OVER

Crash!

Lydia accidentally knocked over a tower of bowls as Martha elbowed past her in a snit.

Bang, clang!

Metal trays, flung from the storage shelf, hit the kitchen table as Martha does what Mary was supposed to do.

R-E-E-E-e-e-r!

The cat unwisely left his tail in Martha's path as she carried more food to the dining area.

There, she tried to get Mary's attention. Useless. Mary looked at no one but Jesus, and He seemed to be deliberately avoiding eye contact with Martha—even though she, with dramatic effect, plunked the heaviest platter of food right between the two of them.

If I can't get them to see me, I'll make them hear me!

In the kitchen again, Martha slammed pans together. She

stomped back and forth between the cooking and serving areas, tight-lipped, glaring, and exhaling loudly with each angry breath. In the kitchen again, Martha whacked a large knife against a hapless legume as loudly as possible on the cutting board. Martha stoked herself into a fuming, fussing, force of nature. She became a walking whirlwind.

A Prophet Without Honor

Let me reinforce something from the previous chapter: "The core value and greatest personal wealth in Mediterranean cultures is honor. . . . A person or group that loses honor is as good as dead. . . . Appearances are more important than reality. . . . Sometimes it is necessary to attack the honor of another in order to save one's own honor. Publicity is a key element in honor and shame."[4]

Get the picture?

Rabbis forbade women to be schooled in the law,[5] and yet Jesus allowed Mary to sit under His instruction—possibly with religious teachers from Jerusalem (or those who reported to them) looking on. Mary was, in effect, acting like a man—an *appallingly* dishonorable thing in that time and place. To further catastrophize matters, Mary shamed herself not in a corner of the room, but right at everyone's focal point. We all know how tongues will wag in a small town.

Imagine Martha's horror. What may have gone through her mind?

I can't believe Mary is sitting there—right at His feet! How can she do that? How can Jesus let her do that? Everyone is staring. Some of them are already whispering. Soon the whole village will know.

I don't know what to do.

Never has anyone shamed our family as Mary is doing now. Jesus acts as if it's perfectly normal for Mary to sit there. We may never recover from this.

I feel sick.

Why doesn't He say something? Do something? I can't stand it. Mary's honor is gone, but it's not too late to recover Jesus' honor. If He won't save Himself, I'll do it for Him.

It probably never occurred to Martha that all the shame was hers.

A Woman Without a Clue

At this point, Martha has not recognized Jesus as Messiah, the Son of God. (That comes later, just before He resurrects her brother in John 11.) To her, He may have been merely the most interesting prophet of late; the most "famous" person to visit her village; or just a typical man who had no idea what was obviously wrong or how to fix it.

This explains why she addressed Him as "Lord" (with little *o-r-d,* the same as saying "Sir"). It also explains why she burst upon Him in a sudden manner. (Again, we know this from the Greek word used that means to be present instantly.) Finally, it explains why, when she said, "Don't You care that my sister has left me to serve alone?" that she was essentially accusing Him of being brainless, heartless, or both.

I know that's shocking, but the original language is very strong *and* very clear.[6] Looking at the other times that the same idea of not caring is used in the New Testament adds light. Remember when the disciples were at sea during a storm while Jesus slept in the boat? They said the exact thing Martha said: "Don't You care?" Think of the story Jesus told about a good shepherd caring for his sheep through danger, but a hired hand fleeing because he "doesn't care." Finally, recall Judas's feigned financial concern for the poor when in fact he "didn't care."[7] It's the English equivalent of saying, "He couldn't care less."

Oh, Martha! You will soon know just how much Jesus cares.

A Rebuke Without a Sting

Four times in the New Testament, Jesus repeated someone's name twice. Each time, the subject was in the wrong.[8]

"Simon, Simon . . ."

"Jerusalem, Jerusalem . . ."

"Saul, Saul . . ."

"Martha, Martha . . ."

Culturally, there's a reason for this. Repeating someone's name twice is meant to soften the inevitable scolding; to convey tenderness toward the erring.[9] We do the same thing when we point out someone's blind spot, prefacing it with, "You're a really good friend, *but* . . ."

Elsewhere we read that Jesus loved Martha.[10] The Greek word used there means He loved her *dearly*.[11] His gentle correction of her here, when He could have rightfully lambasted her, proves how *very much* Jesus loved Martha—maxed out and all!

In the original language, Jesus' description of Martha as "worried and troubled about many things" meant something more like this: "Your turbocharged anxiety over a multitude of details has fragmented your life." Really! The Greek word for "troubled" is *turbe* (rhymes with Herbie).[12] It's a root of our English word "turbulence."[13] How would *you* like to be called "turbulent" in front of all your guests—especially when you were trying to be the epitome of gracious hospitality?

NO ROOM FOR DESSERT

The evening did *not* go as Martha had planned.

Her sister not only abandoned her at a crucial time, but also brought shame on herself, the family, and their guests. Now the most honored guest rebuked Martha when all her efforts were for Him. (Well, *some* of her efforts.) It's as if Jesus looked inside Martha and pulled out deep things not even she knew about herself, and then displayed them to everyone.

Desperate for air, for space, Martha escaped into the cool night. She strode to the far side of the house—away from the warm lamplight spilling from the windows, away from the lively music lacing the breeze. She found a stone bench near a fountain in their moonlit garden, and she sat. Her feet bumped something under the bench and she picked it up—the new brass platter that Mary was supposed to have used in the kitchen. *Will that girl ever learn?*

Thoughts of Mary led to thoughts of Jesus. His rebuke circled through Martha's mind, repeated in her ears, and churned in her heart. She had not planned on hearing something like that! But He wasn't cruel. Martha wasn't even sure that anyone else heard what Jesus said to her.

He's right, though. I am anxious. I do feel that my life is in pieces. But what else can I do? I have certain responsibilities. A reputation. Other people to think of besides myself.

Rain clouds drifted in front of the moon. The deepening darkness suited Martha.

Maybe some are born to study and prayer. The rest of us take care of the business of life. Someone has to! It's what I've always done. It's what I was made for.

After several moments, the wind picked up and bright moonlight again found Martha. She considered her shadowy, blurred image in the brass platter.

If I didn't know better, I'd say this is Mary's reflection.

SPECIALTY OF THE HOUSE

One thing.

Jesus told Martha that's all that was truly essential.

If that were all we had on our plates, we'd think we had it made! Life would be *so easy* if we had only to do one thing. We'd have tons of spare time in which we could learn to paint and to speak a foreign language; to plant a garden, write a book, and refinish the kitchen cabinets—but then we'd be back to overloaded schedules and maxed-out lifestyles.

One thing.

Jesus said this is what Mary chose.

He would've been justified to command Hurricane Martha, "Shut up and sit down! You need to hear this, too." The result? Stingy outward compliance. I guarantee, though Martha might have sat down on the outside, she would've been standing up on the inside. No, I don't think posture is the point here.

One thing.

Jesus equated it with "the good part."

Isn't attending to life's details good? Isn't taking care of other people good? Isn't being absorbed in ministry good? None can realistically be abandoned for the sake of dreamy introspection. That's not practical.

One thing.

Jesus said it wouldn't be taken away.

Oh, great! So that means, then, all the things we've worked and sacrificed for will be taken away? That it's all been for nothing?

One thing.

What is it? I want an answer, and I want it now.

CARRY OUT

Often, looking at the original language will illuminate a Scripture passage. In this case, the Greek word for "one thing" means (drum roll, please) "one thing." (Rim shot.)

How hard can it be to track what Jesus meant? I wanted to cross this mystery off my list and go on with my life. Grumblingly, I searched commentaries. "One thing" means only one kind of food was needed. "One thing" means simplicity. "One thing" means to achieve contemplation. "One thing" means to worship. "One thing" means to submit to Christ's authority. "One thing" means to sit at Jesus' feet.

Can "one thing" mean all of these things?

None of these things?

Then it hit me. (Ouch!) Mary knew what it was, because she chose it. This means she had to have been able to identify it from other choices. If I acted like Mary, maybe I'd be able to spot the "one thing" and choose it, too.

So I did.

For about twenty years now, since the peak of my worka-holism, I've been sitting and listening. Somewhere along the way, I stopped being obsessed with defining "one thing" into a specific task to perform and evaluate. And I also learned this: Sitting wasn't the "one thing," but the "one thing" made Mary sit. Listening wasn't the "one thing" either, but the "one thing" made Mary listen.

Maybe the Greek "one thing" is intentionally vague for a reason. Perhaps "one thing" is not a thing to do, but a way to be; not a place to go, but a place to begin.

CHAPTER FIVE

It's Not Just Me: Meet My Martha Buddies

The one-and-a-half story, white frame house where I grew up sat on a shady half acre just outside a midsized, Midwestern town.

If you and I could visit in person right now, I'd show you pictures of my older brother—Steve—and me from the early 1960s. Standing in front of a silver foil Christmas tree. Standing in front of huge inflatable Easter bunnies. Standing in front of birthday cakes. Standing in front of the new doghouse. Based on those images alone, you might think we had a boring childhood. *Au contraire, bon ami!* Where else but in the Bible Belt could kids baptize kittens in the sump? Rope moving cars off a blacktop country road? Jump out of the tree house naked? Leap off dresser tops onto crayon-targeted bedsheets? Put lipstick on the tomcat? All true stories.

Remembering this, I concluded that any early memory involving my brother also involves *rule breaking*. I also remembered that any early memory of playing alone involves *list making*.

When I played teacher, I made lists of students and designed charts for recording grades.

When I played nurse, I made lists of my patients and designed charts of their vital signs and diseases.

When I played mommy, I made lists of the errands I had to do and recorded all of my baby doll's milestones in a secondhand baby book with then-singer-idol Bobby Sherman named as the father. (No, he doesn't know. Some things are better left unsaid.)

Then I discovered shoeboxes.

In elementary school, I collected discarded shoeboxes to use as drawer dividers and shelf organizers. The detailed chore-charts I made to earn an allowance thrilled my parents until they realized I was only interested in making the charts, not doing the chores.

In high school, I made it my goal to ace every test and be involved in every extracurricular activity except sports since, like most other Type A's, I hated grime and sweat. A cappella choir, drama, yearbook, marching band. (Which reminds me: If you must store your overloaded purse in your busby-style band hat, remember to loosen the chin strap accordingly lest the reduced intake of oxygen to your brain cause you to turn left instead of right at the coda of "Billy, Don't Be a Hero" and march alone toward the opposite end zone during the homecoming halftime performance. Not that it ever happened to me.) My term papers exceeded my teachers' expectations. Awards for academic achievement filled my scrapbook. I excelled in overcommitment more than organization. Too bad the school didn't offer a lettering program for Future Workaholics of America with a variety of medals to earn. It would have been nice to have had *something* on my chest in those days.

In college, I overcommitted again, but this time, I was organized! By the second day of class, a chronological list of all semester projects hung above my desk. I got a buzz out of highlighting completed tasks and shocking my instructors by turning in assignments months early.

Was I the only one to do these things? Do all Type A, perfectionistic women have early childhood memories of this nature? Is Marthaness hereditary or is it forged by one's environment? Are manifestations of perfectionistic behavior triggered by internal crises? These questions demand in-depth, objective, authoritative answers. Too bad I don't have any.*

Instead, I've conducted a totally unscientific survey of my Martha Buddies, which yielded inconclusive findings—but, hey, the cheesecake was great and I got to write it off as a business expense. You'll meet six of them now. In upcoming chapters, they'll share with you again about motherhood, careers, cleaning binges, and more. By the end of the book, I hope you'll feel you made seven new friends who understand the struggles of naturally being a Martha to the max!

LET THE BUDDIES BEGIN

As I spoke with each of my maxed-out friends, I noticed something interesting. Though we may be maxed out in varying degrees, we *like* our personalities. None of us said anything close to, "How I wish my perfectionism would go away! How I long for a lackadaisical temperament! How I yearn for a mint julep!" Our Martharisms endear us to ourselves, and we wouldn't want to swap traits with anyone.

We're not alone in liking our obsessive-compulsive personalities. A university study on perfectionists included this observation: "Many people we interviewed came to us not knowing whether they were being diagnosed as having a problem, or being congratulated for having high standards. . . . We found a whole range of people who were happy with being perfectionists and people who were quite distressed by it. However, none of them were willing to give it up."[1]

On a more personal level, every employer in my work history commended me for perfectionistic qualities: tireless work ethic, attention to details, and personal sacrifice for the business's greater good. Going back even further, all my teachers praised my schoolwork. The added extras I provided that no one else thought of (such as building a cotton gin out of tongue depressors for our study of American inventors) filled them with awe and me with pride.

• All right, all right. You and my editor both deserve a token serious answer or two. Skip ahead to chapter 7 if you want.

When I first met Lynn, she immediately conveyed warmth and openness, so I instantly classified her as a Type B Mary. But the day I saw her ring binders, I knew I'd met a kindred spirit.

She invited me to see her recently remodeled home office (she taught computer to grade school kids) and, I declare, when I saw her labeled notebooks lining tidy shelves, I heard music. I felt connected. If you like crafts, this probably happens to you when you see sock bunnies, calico bears, or folk stenciling in someone's home. If you're into antiques, you feel this way when you see Depression glass in a vintage china cabinet. If you're into junk, you feel this way when you see an Elvis painting on black velvet.

Lynn remembers one particular Type A, Martha instance from her high school years. I'd love to tell you about it, but Lynn wanted to control this anecdote, so below is her story verbatim.

★　★　★

As a military kid, I swung it so we could have our high school prom at the base officer's club. When I ran into resistance from the chef, who didn't want to do things exactly the way I wanted to, I pulled rank on him. Puffed up in all my "Chairperson of the Junior Senior Prom Committee" regality, I called my peer, Colonel So-and-So, the base commander. After listening intently to my grievances, the colonel thanked me for my insights and hung up. His next call was to my father, a sergeant who was soon standing at attention in the colonel's office, getting a very pointed lesson on keeping one's children in line. Needless to say, I immediately fell to the bottom of the food chain.

★　★　★

Don't you love that! Imagine Lynn, the ink on her driver's license still wet, boldly marching around a base of the world's mightiest military power, fully expecting her commands to be obeyed. Talk about Martha to the max! From that day on, I'm sure the mere sight of her ignited cries of "Incoming!" She probably earned her own little blip on their radar screen, too.

Now consider Teri. Another Martha-friend of mine, she and I share a lifelong love of books. Another link in our friendship was formed when I discovered she did the same no-no I do on occasion: We excuse ourselves from dinner guests under false pretenses to read in secret just one more chapter of a gripping page-turner. Here's how she describes her childhood Marthaness.

★　　★　　★

When I was in grade school, my dad built me a bookshelf of my very own in my room and I began filling it full of books. I decided the books needed to be organized in some way, so I alphabetized them by author and title. After doing this, I decided there needed to be some way to index the books, so I used a 3" x 5" card box and began making a card catalog by title, author, and subject of my books.

★　　★　　★

Now why did Teri Jo think her books needed to be shelved according to a system? Other kids might've been satisfied by arranging them from the tallest to the shortest. Or by grouping all the books by color. Or just getting them off the floor. Ladies and gentlemen of the jury, I submit to you that little Teri alphabetized and indexed her books because of her Type A, Martha temperament! I rest my case.

Lori and her husband live in a beautiful log home in the Colorado Rockies and have three children, whom they homeschool. Lori also, by the way, offers her guests only the best ice cream: Breyers! (Shameless attempt to get corporate sponsoring and lifetime supply of free ice cream for both of us. Make mine chocolate.)

★　　★　　★

I remember my sense of order [from as early as] first grade. I kept careful track of the books on my homemade list. I, to this day, still love all of my lists. When I can see my life on paper, I feel so much better! As a child, I always had lists. Lists of gifts I was going to give people, my own Christmas list, lists of my best friends and their addresses and phone numbers . . . lists, lists, lists!

★　　★　　★

Sheryl is a single mom from the West Coast who has taught on three continents, done professional modeling, earned two master's degrees, and is the top administrator at a private-care facility. You might think her earliest memory of wanting order would involve organizational flow charts, performance standards, or health codes, but it doesn't. It has to do with socks.

★   ★   ★

My earliest memory of displaying my Type A behavior was being stressed out as a kid over my sister's messiness! She didn't need a sock drawer because she built piles of socks all around our shared bedroom. To me, a drawer for the socks was very important. It didn't really matter to me what the drawer looked liked on the inside. The socks just had to make it into the drawer. Chaos could reign on the inside of the drawer, but heaven forbid, not in the room where anyone could see it.

★   ★   ★

Another Type A, Martha to the max is Deanna. She's single, travels internationally in youth ministry, and also teaches high school Spanish. Deanna's Type A, Martha-traits range from organizing her crayons in rainbow order in grade school to choosing courses in college that had structure and pattern, like accounting and foreign languages. She recalls a summer trip to Spain, where she visited the Museo del Prado, one of the most prestigious museums in the world.

★   ★   ★

I sat there listening to descriptions of the use of light and dark, etc., and just thought, Well, it'd look ugly hanging above my fireplace! *The research paper I had to write for that course was the only C I received on anything in college.*

★   ★   ★

Poor Deanna! She still managed to pull a 4.0 every semester, but that C on useless abstract stuff marred her otherwise-perfect college transcript.

Now meet Shawnee. She and her newlywed husband live in a small apartment in a small town where he pastors a small church on a small budget. But Shawnee is a big dreamer and storyteller extraordinaire.

★　　★　　★

During college I worked the supper shift in our school cafe-teria. One night as I was cleaning up, I noticed that I had lined up all the leftover gelatin bowls according to color and type. I asked my boss [about it] and she said, "Yeah, you do that every night. Beats me why because it doesn't make a bit of difference to the Jell-O."

I went back to my dorm room and found that although my closet was color-coordinated, I couldn't see the carpet in my room for all the clothes thrown on the floor. And although my class notes were completely organized, the majority of my as-signments came back with something along the lines of "This would have been an A paper if you'd only turned it in during the right semester."

It wasn't that I didn't try to turn things in on time, it was just that I was so busy coming up with more organized methods of study or presentation that I forgot I even had a deadline.

★　　★　　★

Did you see yourself in any of these stories? There's nothing I'd like better than to hear about your early experiences with Marthaness, especially if quality cheesecake is involved.

Let's imagine that you are joining me and my six Martha Bud-dies at this charming coffee shop I sometimes escape to called the Whistlestop. It's in the old part of a nearby smaller town, right across from the train station. The inside walls are old brick, the wooden floors creak, and the aroma of coffee and chocolate fills the air. High painted shelves display baskets, pottery, gift tins, leafy plants, and old books. Acoustic music plays softly in the back-ground. We'll have to push two tables together, being careful not to take those that the regulars sit at every afternoon to read their newspapers and play checkers.

Now for the big question: Which Martha Buddy do you want to sit across from?

— Is it Lynn, who expressed her Marthaness by presuming authority she didn't have?
— Perhaps you connected with Teri, who took scrupulous care of her belongings.
— Maybe you're eager to share with Lori your partiality for listing things on paper.
— Single mom or not, you can sit across from Sheryl and talk about how you savor neat surroundings.
— If cutesy stories and "what ifs" bore you, join Deanna for a conversation that focuses on facts, not feelings. (But guard your plate if there's anything chocolate on it; her fork is fast!)
— If you like to create elaborate plans for projects better than doing the projects themselves, count on a lively discussion with Shawnee.
— And if you're especially maxed out, sit right across from me.

FROM PLEASURE TO PAIN . . . AND BACK AGAIN

I had natural childbirth.

Now you may be thinking, *Big deal!* because you did, too. Now the competitive-spirited Marthas at our table who have given birth will start one-up-mom-ship on each other.

"I was in labor for twelve hours."

"That's nothing! I was in pain for thirty-six hours during a snowstorm."

"Ha! I can top that! My water broke on a Thursday and I didn't deliver my matching nine-pound twins until the next Tuesday."

Maybe you're silently blessing whoever invented that thing called an epidural. But you have to understand why even saying that I had natural childbirth is such a big deal for me: I am a *wimp.*

Yes, I know it seems odd for an overbearing, get-out-of-my-way Martha to be a wimp regarding pain, but I am. I can't even rip an adhesive bandage off my arm without pacing around the house and groaning in anticipation of the hair-pulling assault I'm about to suffer. Usually I take the coward's way out and soak the silly thing off in the bathtub.

The direction we're going together in this book is sort of like that adhesive bandage on my arm. Sometimes the quirky control-things we do are covering up a hurt or fear of some kind. Or maybe not. But the only way to tell is to pull the bandage back and look—and I promise I won't yank it off, with or without warning. I much prefer a nice, long soak in a warm humor book.

Perfectionism is not always a pretty sight. But you know what? Wherever there's a hurt, there's an open door for healing. Jesus loved Martha just as much as He loved Mary. Jesus also loves _us_ as much as our first-century counterparts—as is and maxed out! As we learn more about ourselves, we'll discover exciting truths, one of which is that the Lord doesn't want Marthas to stop being Marthas and all become Marys. Instead, He wants us to use our God-given gifts in healthier and happier ways than ever before.

Since we've confirmed through this chapter (and our imaginary meeting at the Whistlestop) that our penchant for perfection is lifelong, let's move ahead and explore its possible sources. Is it strictly heredity? Environment? Talk-show hogwash or divine truth?

Most important, the next time we're all at the Whistlestop, will someone else pick up the tab?

CHAPTER SIX

The Martha of the New Millennium

In our culture, women who roared feminine empowerment in the 1970s ("I want it all!") yawned feminine exhaustion in the 1980s ("I need a nap!"). This is the era in which the term *Type E* was coined because the Type A label could no longer contain us. In her 1986 book *The Type E Woman,* clinical psychologist Harriet Braiker described the pressures of women who feel they must do and be everything to everyone. Two years later, Ellen Sue Stern wrote *The Indispensable Woman.* Am I a "Type I" woman? Are you? Stern says indispensability is proven by "making yourself overly available and accessible . . . whether you have the time, energy, or inclination."[1]

The 1990s' solution to all this do-it-all, all-the-time crisis was "sequencing." This allowed women to alternate their focus between work and home for specific periods. As wonderful, sensible, and balanced as sequencing sounds, it still worries me. Not only does it mean we can drag out stress over our entire lifetime instead of a mere thirty or forty years, it also implies that by the time we die, we *should have* done it all—and done it well.

Are we really making progress here?

OUT ON A LIMB

I don't believe in reincarnation. Unless, of course, we're talking about the fashion industry. It has a knack for declaring whatever I finally purged from my closet as the "must-have wardrobe centerpiece" of the new season. Not that I could find arch supports for my go-go boots anyway. But as far as cosmic soul recycling goes, I don't buy it.

I do, however, agree with King Solomon that there is nothing new under the sun, including being maxed out.

Christian women today identify with Martha of Bethany probably more than any other biblical character. (When's the last time *you* said, "Queen Esther and I have so much in common!") This instant sisterhood with Martha is especially amazing since she appears so few times in Scripture. Even so, I constantly hear Christian women echo, "I'm *such* a Martha!"

Why are you and I the Marthas of the New Millennium?

Because as perfectionistic Christian women, we think, feel, and act as Martha did—overburdened and underappreciated. We have high standards, low energy, little time, and no tolerance. Chronically on the edge of burnout, we're too tired to keep going, but too afraid to stop. In spite of being labeled overcommitted, we still feel we *need to, ought to, should do* even more for our families, our careers, our churches, and our communities. In fact, we may think that if we tried really, really hard, we could stop continental drift.

The only plate shifting Martha of Bethany knew had to do with pottery. Still, in her time and in her world, she was maxed out! What would she and her sister Mary be like in our millennium? Here's how I imagine they might behave in a scenario most of us have lived through at least once.

MARY AND MARTHA ATTEND A WOMEN'S RETREAT
IN TEN SIMPLE STEPS

Step 1

Mary: Receives brochure. Likes the pretty colors. Thinks the women pictured look like they'll be fun to talk to.

Martha: Receives brochure. Circles typographical errors.

Step 2

Mary: Calls friends and convinces them all to go as a group and share a room.

Martha: Reads qualifications of speakers to see if they're worth the cost.

Step 3

Mary: Checks her calendar and discovers she's supposed to be at Church Clean up Day instead. Calls the coordinator to back out, but feels really, truly, awfully bad about it (for at least fifteen seconds).

Martha: As coordinator, receives calls from several women backing out of Church Clean up Day. Spends two hours on the phone finding replacements.

Step 4

Mary: Registers for retreat by phone, hoping as she reads her charge card number aloud that she hasn't exceeded the credit limit. Exhilarated from accomplishing so much in one day, gathers an assortment of snacks and board games to take along.

Martha: Using the Internet, prints out a map showing the quickest route to the retreat, plus a description of its typical climate during that season. After studying the list of activities on the brochure, makes a list of wardrobe choices (with coordinated accessories) to fit every change in temperature or humidity. Double-checks cosmetics suitcase, which is routinely stocked with travel-sized toiletries and her medical information typed neatly on an index card. After balancing her checkbook to the penny, she completes and mails her registration, paying extra for a private room.

Step 5

Mary: Arrives with her friends late at the retreat because during each of their frequent pit stops, they bought little gifts for loved ones at home, chatted in the bathrooms, and took goofy snapshots of each other as if they were all teenagers again.

Martha: Arrives alone at the retreat right on time, proud to have completed her church obligations before she left on her nonstop, record-setting road trip.

Step 6

Mary: Stays up late that night playing games and swapping stories with her roommates. Before she falls asleep, resets her alarm clock for an hour later, having decided she can skip shampooing her hair and just wear her Mickey Mouse ball cap the next day instead.

Martha: Stays up late that night keying and cross-referencing notes from the speaker's workshops into her laptop computer. Checks and rechecks her alarm clock to make sure she has enough time in the morning to be properly costumed and coifed before anyone sees her.

Step 7

Mary: Sleeps deeply and well all night.
Martha: Has trouble falling asleep; mind races with reminders of how she must wake up early.

Step 8

Mary: Sees Martha across the table at breakfast, furrows her brow, and thinks, *That woman is so uptight . . . I wonder if I should buy more cheesy-doodles for the trip home?*

Martha: Sees Mary across the table at breakfast, arches her brow, and thinks, *That woman is admiring me, but I wouldn't be caught in public looking like her unless I'd just had major surgery.*

Step 9

Mary: Shares with her class at church the next Sunday what a wonderful time of fellowship was had by all at the retreat and how she can't wait for the next one.

Martha: Apologizes to her class at church the next Sunday that she did not have time to prepare a multimedia presentation and humbly offers instead crisp photocopies of her transcribed notes from the retreat for those who couldn't attend (Or, she thinks to herself while looking at Mary, *for those who were there but didn't pay attention*).

Step 10

Mary: As usual, is among the last to leave the church because she spends so much time talking with people afterwards. Before she goes, she takes a quiet moment to sit alone in the sanctuary. There, she meditates on God's love for her and how He expressed it by refreshing her spirit at the retreat and deepening her friendships with other women.

Martha: As usual, is among the last to leave the church because as the coordinator of several ministries, she always finds urgent paperwork in her church mailbox. Before she leaves, she sits alone in the church office to update her personal planner with details for upcoming committee meetings. Feeling that familiar tight anxiety in her stomach, Martha concludes that the women's retreat failed to "refresh and restore" her as its brochure promised. Since demanding a refund wouldn't be the Christian thing to do, she decides to coordinate a better retreat herself and jots a note to the pastor telling him the date she has selected for it.

OK, you're right. I can't guarantee that Mary and Martha would act *exactly* that way in our contemporary culture. But I can guarantee that if you're a Martha of the New Millennium, you saw at least a little of yourself in the women's retreat scenario. I know I did. But what's wrong with that? After all, we're just being ourselves—busy, in control, overcommitted, judgmental, perfectionistic (somebody stop me!), demanding, Type A, obsessive-compulsive Christian women. This over-the-edge uptightness transcends all cultures and spans all epochs. Now, there's a surefire slogan for a high-tech girdle. Instead of "One size fits all," it's "Spans all epochs." If only the Martha temperament was as accommodating!

A MARTHA BY ANY OTHER NAME

We know there are different types of people and that they naturally cluster together in their own cozy groups. It doesn't matter what you label them, either. Jocks and dweebs. Motorheads and yuppies. Liberals and conservatives. Marys and Marthas.

What would happen if you announced to those groups that the way they are is *wrong?* That they must become the opposite of themselves? There would be an uproar! A coup! (I'd make the announcement myself, but I don't look good in traction.)

When I began to fathom the fallout of Marthaness on both myself and the survivors around me, I knew I had to fix it. But the only solution seemed to be changing myself into a Mary. Ugh! She was a wishy-washy, starry-eyed, cream puff compared to Martha. A weakling! But apparently, for some reason, that's what pleased the Lord, so that's the kind of woman I would have to be. Never mind that Maryness was totally against my nature. She was the sister who received praise, so that made her my new role model. It also made me miserable.

I remember extending my personal quiet time each day. This was my token "sitting at the feet of Jesus" routine, which I assumed then was the "one thing" Jesus spoke of to Martha. I had not yet discovered that the "one thing" was not a thing to do, but a way to be; not a place to go, but a place to begin. Back then, my body may have been sitting still, but my mind was racing! Did I really think God had no idea that I was antsy? That I resented this requirement and counted the minutes until it was over?

"See me, Lord? *(Take turkey out of freezer.)* See me sitting here at Your feet? *(Buy postage stamps, get tires on car rotated.)* See me read my Bible and pray? *(Reschedule kids' dental appointments. There are cobwebs in that corner . . .)* I'm doing the Mary thing, aren't I? *(My toe itches.)* This is 'the good part,' the 'one thing,' isn't it?" Then zoom! I could cross that chore off my list and get to more pleasant things, like cleaning storm windows or preparing for a tax audit.

That approach still left me feeling frazzled and empty. Maybe the key was in being Mary all day rather than just at its beginning. Double ugh! But if that was what Jesus wanted, I supposed I could at least try. Besides, a good friend had often reminded me: "PAMITP." This stands for "People Are More Important Than Projects." That sounded like a Mary thing to me, so I adopted that as my new motto. I was all set to be a blessing to the lucky people around me.

For this phase, I postponed all my projects and chores until I was absolutely, totally sure that all the people in my life had been talked to (nicely), listened to (patiently), fed (healthily), and put to bed (finally!). *Then* I let the Martha in me come out and get at those projects I'd been thinking about all day but hadn't done. The nice part about this was I had zero interruptions. The bad part was I had to sacrifice a little thing called *sleep.*

The result? I spent less time on projects, more time with people, and was getting crankier every day. Hmm. That wasn't working either. What was the problem! What was the "one thing"?

During my transition months between Martha and Mary, I read these words: "You can always drift into being a Martha. All you have to do is just let yourself go. No woman ever drifted into being a Mary."[2] Hey, I knew all about letting myself go. That's the quickest route to being maxed out! But what was the way into being a Mary? "Drift" nothin'! I tried *marching* there and couldn't make it. What was I doing wrong?

DOING . . . DOING . . . *DUH!*

Some of my teachers from college had pet phrases. When one wanted to refer to someone's certain doom he would say, "It'll be flowers and slow music for him." Another couldn't resist making puns as he talked about ancient tribes from the Old Testament: "the Canaanites, the Jebusites, the Hittites, and the Chigger Bites. No, scratch that last one." And still another responded to class questions with, "The answer is always in the text. Look in the text."

So, it was back to the text I went to discover what I was doing wrong in my pursuit to be like Mary. I opened my Bible to Luke 10:38–42 and read again:

> Now it happened as they went that He entered a certain village; and a certain woman named Martha welcomed Him into her house. And she had a sister called Mary, who also sat at Jesus' feet and heard His word. But Martha was distracted with much serving, and she approached Him and said, "Lord, do You not care that my sister has left me to serve alone? Therefore tell her to help me." And Jesus answered and said to her, "Martha, Martha, you are worried and troubled about many things. But one thing is needed, and Mary has chosen that good part, which will not be taken away from her."

What did Mary *do?*

1. She sat at Jesus feet. (Yeah, yeah. I did that. What's next?)
2. She heard His words. (Yeah, yeah. I've heard a million sermons in my life. What else?)
3. She chose the good part.

And there it was. Not the whole answer to what the "one thing" was, but a major stepping-stone that brought me closer than I had ever been before.

How could I have missed it? Because, like Martha, I was distracted.

"There was a time in Mary's life when she had made a choice, and Martha had not. That is the difference. Mary had chosen, and that is always the difference between the person who is satisfied with Christ and the person who is dissatisfied with life."[3] A large part of my problem wasn't in what I was *doing,* but in what I was *choosing.*

PAPER OR PLASTIC?

Everybody sees one day end and another begin. Big deal. Ditto with weeks and months and years. Not many people, though, get to straddle two centuries. Even fewer, two millennia.*

But when you think of how endless eternity is, a millennium —a thousand years!—is a flash in the pan. Even less, a century. Compared to that big picture, the countless choices we make every day seem, well, trivial. Almost pointless.

Take going to the grocery store. Does it really matter if we wear old jeans or a new dress? If we buy large or small curd cottage cheese? If we tote our groceries home in plastic bags or paper ones?**

Besides, we Marthas are better at giving orders than making choices. Even deciding which errands to do (or not do) during our lunch hour is hard for us. We want to do them all! Jesus said, "Only one thing is needful." Marthas think, "But many things are *ought*-ful!" Every minute to us has option-overload. We *ought to* do this, and this, and this, and this, and this, and this, and this.

We're moving closer to finding the "one thing." But in the meantime, there's a tool to help us find the best choice out of many.

---

* The whole Y2K frenzy turned out to be a nonevent. No power outages. No looting. No WWIII. Even now, months later, my family has barely made a dent in our Cup-O-Noodles stockpile.

** If you're an environmentally conscious Martha to the max, you probably made your own reusable bags from organic-cotton canvas and then hand-stenciled nature designs on them with soy-based ink. But you only get points for this if you either bicycle to the store or go by mule. Driving pollutes the air, thus negating your conservation efforts.

WWMD?

There's a fad now that I hope sticks around for a long time. It's the "WWJD?" stuff. We see it on T-shirts, wristbands, bumper stickers, book covers, coffee mugs, and even engraved in wedding bands. The letters stand for, "What would Jesus do?" This was the ultimate question by which every choice was measured in Charles Sheldon's classic book *In His Steps.**

That's what we need. Some sort of measuring device by which all our choices and *ought to's* could be separated into good and bad, right and wrong. Wouldn't that be freeing? Think of all the pressure and guilt that would relieve! Think of all the time and energy that would save!

Mary had just such a filter.

Today, we'd use the word *focus*. It was for lack of focus that Martha was distracted (literally, without traction). It's hard to focus on anything when our vision is constantly sweeping many things. That's like spending our lives on the Tilt-a-Whirl.

The best corrective lens to bring focus is the eternal perspective. Paul wrote, "We fix our eyes not on what is seen, but on what is unseen. For what is seen is temporary, but what is unseen is eternal."[4] Mary didn't have the New Testament to teach her this, but she did have personal observation of watching what Jesus did. Perhaps He even quoted to her the Old Testament equivalent of Paul's quote.

> Lord, make me to know my end,
> And what is the measure of my days,
> That I may know how frail I am. . . .
> Certainly every man at his best is but vapor. . . .
> Surely they busy themselves in vain.[5]

The litmus test, then, for choosing what to focus on is a simple question: "In light of eternity, how much does this matter?"

---

* If we don't want to spend this millennium as maxed out as we were in the last one, maybe we should ask, "What would Martha do?" and then do just the opposite.

Martha answered that question by continuing to flit from one temporal detail to another. Mary answered it by sitting at the feet of Jesus.

Whether it's for a millennium or a single moment, focus is essential. When our focus is based on eternity, it won't roar empowerment nor will it yawn exhaustion.

It will sing freedom.

CHAPTER SEVEN

Personality Type or Hype?

Do you have any idea how many books there are on personality?
Me neither.

But it's probably a huge number that not even a perfectionist
like me could track down, in spite of incurring excessive on-line
fees, long-distance charges, and the ire of several librarians in the
reference department. And if you've never seen a librarian's ire, let
me tell you, it's not a pretty sight.

Anyway, this whole chapter on the origin and burgeoning
repercussions of personality typing tried to get away from me several times. Sort of like a gargantuan undersea squid covered in
slime escaping from a sparkly size six evening dress and matching
shoes. The reason for this is threefold: (1) The field of typology is
growing every hour; (2) my perfectionism wanted to master it all
from the first smiley face scrawled on a cave wall to the latest test-

ing instruments on the Internet and then present them concisely for you here; and (3) gargantuan undersea squid are allergic to sequins.

There are hundreds—nay, thousands—of personality titles, tests, audio- and videocassettes, seminars, workbooks, quizzes, and commentaries. The glory of that is that if we don't like the results of one test, we can simply declare it invalid and take a different one. The shame of it is that self-testing can become yet another addiction and lead to an obsession with typing ourselves.

Therefore, I present to you now a capsule of personality study, not in chronological order (why take the easy way out?), but from the most *complex* to the most *simple.*

A COMPREHENSIVE OVERVIEW
OF PERSONALITY TYPING (SORT OF)

Before the 1920s, personality analysis was usually done only on the mentally ill. This should be our first clue. Then, in the late 1920s through the early 1940s, American psychologist William Moulton Marston invented the first polygraph, wrote a book called *The Emotions of Normal People,* designed a temperament test, and created the Wonder Woman comic strip.[1] The temperament test used four factors: Dominance (D), Influence (I), Steadiness (S), and Compliance (C). The DISC method was used to recruit military personnel for World War II. Afterward, it was used in business settings. With four factors being measured, how many possible outcomes do you think there might be? Four? Sixteen? Sixty-four? Try *1 million.*[2] This makes perfect sense when you remember that our government used it. I think of it as an endless, all-you-can-obsess smorgasbord.

Also in the 1940s, the Myers-Briggs Type Indicator (MBTI) surfaced, based on Swiss psychiatrist Carl Jung's theory of human personality.[3] It has four dimensions. The first is Extroversion (E) or Introversion (I). The second is Sensing (S) or Intuition (N). The third is Thinking (T) or Feeling (F). The fourth is Judging (J) or Perceiving (P). Far from having a million possible outcomes like DISC does, MBTI has only sixteen: ISTJ, ISTP, ESTP, ESTJ, ISFJ,

ISFP, ESFP, ESFJ, INFJ, INFP, ENFP, ENFJ, INTJ, INTP, ENTP and ENTJ. I don't know about you, but I'm not thrilled about being labeled with a temperament that could be mistaken for a cable television station.

Narrower still are the four temperaments with which most of us are familiar: sanguine, choleric, melancholy, and phlegmatic. Some say the earliest origins of these are in astrology and the occult.[4] (Ooo!) We do know that Hippocrates used these terms but linked them to bodily fluids that influenced behavior. (Ick!) Popular Christian authors Tim LaHaye and Florence Littauer have written scads of respective best-sellers on temperaments using Hippocrates's four categories, but both broke the link between bodily fluids and behavior.*

Based on these four categories, my ministry co-worker Teresa, whom you met in the first chapter, possessed strong choleric traits, which included take-charge decisiveness ("Do it now"). I possessed strong melancholy traits, which included detailed perfectionism ("Do it right").

More recently, best-selling Christian authors Gary Smalley and John Trent modified Hippocrates's categories into the animal-based temperament descriptions of otter (playful), lion (take charge), beaver (detail-oriented) and golden retriever (loyal).[5] Teresa roared, I gnawed sticks, and we both needed distemper shots.

But even with these last two instruments, we have four possible personality categories and that's twice as many as we all-or-nothing Martha-thinkers need.

THE A'S HAVE IT

In the 1970s, two prestigious names rang forth with a new message. No, it wasn't Sonny and Cher. It wasn't Simon and Garfunkle. It was Friedman and Rosenman. Concluding that the world had folk tunes aplenty, these two medical researchers turned their attention to the relationship between personality traits and

---

* Although there may be merit in the "water retention-PMS thing," which Mr. Male-Doctor-Hippocrates conveniently overlooked.

heart disease.[6] With them originated the labels of Type A and Type B personalities. Friedman and Rosenman said that Type A describes half of all Americans, and that Type B describes forty percent. "The Type A's are the heart-attack prone. They differ from the easygoing, relaxed Type B's in their tendencies to be competitive, achievement oriented, aggressive, hostile, impatient, and driven by the clock."[7]

If Mary and Martha were tested by Friedman and Rosenman, guess which sister would be Type A?

The Type A and Type B labels have survived into this century. Dr. Richard Swenson, author of *Margin* and *The Overload Syndrome,* suggests a variation, though. He describes highly productive people (HPP) and highly sensitive people (HSP).[8]

HPP's	HSP's
Top 10 percent of productivity	Top 10 percent of sensitivity
Accomplish a great deal	Have antennae up for social discord or discomfort
Remarkable work ethic	May seem antisocial
Lack good warning signals	Take longer to heal from social interaction
Have unrealistic standards for others	Often creative
Dole out acceptance based on performance	More susceptible to overload

HPPs typically overload their lives until "there's nothing left to do but crash and burn."[9] HSPs "pay a higher emotional price for almost everything. It is like the world's loudspeaker is always on for them. They wear down more quickly."[10]

Again, if we put Mary and Martha to the HPP/HSP test, guess which sister would be which type?

AND THE POINT IS . . .

From over 1 million personality outcomes with the DISC test to merely two types with the Friedman-Rosenman model, there's an undeniable fact. People love to study themselves!

The problem with that is it can lead to an unhealthy self-absorption. "What do *I* think? What do *I* feel? What do *I* want?" It can also result in virtual written permission to rationalize inappropriate behavior. "Don't expect me to be on time for work—my temperament can't tolerate rigidity!"

Still, just because some people abuse personality tests is not a reason to get rid of them. That's like banning all forms of pain medication because some people become addicted to them—a scary thought for anyone who has had surgery! Used properly, the trustworthy tests have their place and can help us be more considerate of those we live with.[11] I'll never forget how the light bulbs came on for me after attending a group study on temperaments. Someone I'd been butting heads with for years finally made sense! Once I understood more about myself and this other person, I was able to quit being angry at the differences. We both were more understanding and supportive of each other thereafter.

LET'S DO SOMETHING RADICAL

Many of the Marthas I know had a "solid Christian upbringing." As kids, some won awards for Bible quizzing or Scripture memory contests. As young adults, these same Marthas entered Bible college or seminary. There, they probably had to write a personal doctrinal statement (or "Senior Theology Paper") in order to graduate. The professors didn't grade on the curve, either. They used a freight scale. The heavier the finished product, the higher the grade. I received an A+ on mine by coming up with a biblical position for *everything.* "Water is wet," with 1,398 verses to back it up. I graduated feeling that I had mastered the Bible. Familiarity with the Good Book made consulting it seem silly—like hollering "Price check!" in the Everything's-A-Dollar Store.

So I now propose doing something really wild and crazy and

radical. Something you wouldn't have dared, for example, even in your first year of dormitory living when you kidnapped your friend's pet newts, sent her clever ransom notes, and then the whole thing backfired when the newts escaped from your closet and, heading toward the smell of water in the showers, got dried out and stuck in the hall carpet until they were accidentally discovered by someone who foolishly did not wear slippers at night. (Not that it ever happened to me.)

Anyway, the wild and crazy, totally radical thing I propose regarding personality type is to reopen our Bibles and our minds—*at the same time!* That's because personality tests, and even what we believe about them, keep changing. Thus we see the need for an authoritative source that does not change. And no, I do not mean Dick Clark. Not unless we're discussing Top 40 hits.

Assumption #1: God Is the Creator

"In the beginning God created the heavens and the earth"; "By faith we understand that the universe was formed at God's command, so that what is seen was not made out of what was visible"; "You [God] created all things, and by your will they were created and have their being."[12]

So far so good.

Assumption #2: God Loves Everyone the Same

"For the LORD your God is God of gods and Lord of lords, the great God, mighty and awesome, who shows no partiality and accepts no bribes"; "God does not show favoritism"; "[God] is patient with you, not wanting anyone to perish, but everyone to come to repentance."[13]

Still so far so good.

Assumption #3: God Created People Differently

Here's where it gets sticky.

Beginning with the first people to breathe on this planet, God used variety. *Why?* I have no idea—especially because it seems to have brought nothing but trouble.

In Genesis alone is enough personal conflict to fuel a television miniseries for years. Cain and Abel's differences led to the first murder. Ishmael and Isaac became the heads of the Arab-Israeli conflict that continues today. Jacob and Esau's struggles began in the womb and lasted for decades. Joseph's ten older brothers found him so abhorrent that they turned violent. Women weren't exempt from personality conflict, either. Leah and Rachel's rivalry for the affection of their father, and later of their husband, plays like a soap opera.[14]

If you haven't read the entire Bible, let me assure you—human relationships never got any smoother. In the New Testament, even the apostle Paul's close friendship with Barnabas suffered over their sharp disagreement about the compatibility of Mark in their work.[15]

Martha and Mary, also in the New Testament, experienced conflict. Well, OK. Mary may have been oblivious, but Martha had enough conflict for both.

WHAT ABOUT "THEM"?

Daily, we struggle with those whose mind-set, preferences, and priorities clash sharply with ours. It's amazing how many folks there are who actually believe it's OK to toss garbage in the recycling bin without first sterilizing and sorting it. To serve a meal with only three of the four major food groups represented. To wear white shoes and dark pantyhose.

How are we supposed to get along with these . . . these . . . people?

Like marble and thread.

When King Solomon set about to build a temple for God, he required that only skillful workers be used.[16] Materials included logs, iron, and stone. Their strength was needed to provide structure. Also required was fine linen in purple, blue, and crimson. Their softness was needed to add color, quiet, and beauty to inspire worship.

Today, Christ is building His church. Not with cheap, time-efficient concrete blocks, but with people—all kinds of people.[17] Christ selects both the nature and use of each material. Some

Marthas are like priceless marble—solid and able to bear incredible pressure. Some Marys are like fine threads of gold in linen—without them, softness, beauty, and worship would unravel. Both are essential.

Comparing ourselves with others is more than unwise. It is unrighteous.[18]

Paul wrote, "Let us therefore make every effort to do what leads to peace and to mutual edification."[19] Understanding what makes ourselves and others tick *can* foster peace and mutual edification. Judgmental comparison does neither—and that can be done with or without a test.

Let's repeat this silent pledge when we're tempted to get cranky with the Type B Marys in our lives:

> From this day forward, I have released you and all the things about you that are different from me to the sovereignty of God. So go ahead. Wear white shoes and dark pantyhose with my blessing. I promise I won't say a word. (Unless, of course, you're trailing a banner of toilet paper on the bottom of one shoe.)

OK, BUT WHAT ABOUT US?

It's a contradiction to believe that the loving God who created us, saved us, and promised us an abundant life also expects us to live in constant exhaustion, anxiety, and stress. There's no redemption in that. No joy. It's certainly not how Jesus lived.

Somewhere, something went wrong. Our wonderful qualities designed by God for His glory and our good went haywire. Instead of using these gifts according to the manufacturer's instructions, we have, like a blaring pack of Martha Andrettis at the Indy 500 raceway, floorboarded them all.

On the following page is a Martha's Dozen* of traits that have backfired and sent us scrambling to avoid a crash. They illustrate perfectly the observation of Florence Littauer that "a strength taken to an extreme becomes a weakness."

---

* Not to be outdone by some pudgy little baker who adds just one measly doughnut to a dozen, Martha *doubles* hers.

God-given distinction	Maxed-out mannerism
1. ability to notice details	sidetracked by minutia
2. administrative skills	bossiness
3. discernment	uptight judgmentalism
4. affinity for order	nitpicking rigidity
5. goal-oriented	project-obsessed
6. strong work ethic	workaholism
7. heightened sense of responsibility	unending false guilt
8. desire for excellence	perfectionism
9. talent for analyzing and assessing	constant criticizing
10. ability to focus	absorbing tunnel vision
11. capacity to multitask	chronic wheel-spinning
12. perseverance	blindness to limits
13. proper view of self	pride or shame
14. willingness to sacrifice	martyr complex
15. drive to see a project through	burnout
16. optimism to improve things	unrealistic expectations
17. logical thinking	insensitivity to emotions
18. desire for others' happiness	performance trap
19. self-control	stuffed emotions
20. excellent memory	long-term grudges
21. sensitivity to sin	perpetual self-righteousness
22. strong health	intolerance for the weak
23. quick wit	barbed sarcasm
24. independence	isolation

Am I saying, for example, if we have a strong work ethic that we are automatically workaholics? No. I am saying that without constant reliance upon God to use our gifts within healthful boundaries, we can plunge into the stress Martha of Bethany found herself mired in. Then our wonderful, God-given qualities become warped. No longer pearls on a strand, they become links on a heavy chain we were never intended to wear.

*   *   *

Remember Teresa, my former ministry co-worker in chapter 1? She met with me for breakfast recently to talk about our maxed-out former selves, and I toted along this chapter, then still in manuscript form, for her to read. She laughed as she relived our cleaning binge of the storage room.

"Oh! I'd forgotten about the bowling ball!" Teresa said. "And hauling out the trash at night so no one would try to stop us."

"You know," I observed, "it's a wonder we didn't get our pretentious, 'dressed for success' keisters kicked right out the door. Those mellow Type B people we worked with must have thought we were obnoxious—and rightfully so."

She nodded in agreement, "I know! Can you believe we were that uptight?"

"Now it all seems like a bad dream."

Then, as Teresa read the list of maxed-out mannerisms above, she said things like, "Ouch!" "Ooo!" and "Good one!"

After a thoughtful pause, she leaned across the café table and asked, "Debi, were we really that bad?"

"Yep."

"Why?" She leaned closer still. "Why did we push ourselves so hard?"

"Lots of reasons," I said, motioning for the server to refill our coffee cups.

PLEASE PASS THE BLAME

We spent the next half hour or so discussing factors that contributed to our previous maxed-out lifestyles. Of course the usual suspects were rounded up for questioning.

1. *God*	He made us this way.
2. *The devil*	Everything that goes wrong in our lives is part of a satanic plot, including bad hair days.
3. *Our parents*	Because guilt is thicker than water.

4. *The media*	A global conspiracy to undermine civilization as we know it and enslave us to merchandising moguls. Batteries not included.
5. *Popular culture*	Feeds the burn-out-in-a-blaze-of-glory, create-your-own-destiny, have-it-all, be-it-all myth.
6. *The Christian-legalist subculture*	Condemns secular workaholics, but applauds "tireless servants." (But not too much lest those servants become prideful and require church discipline.*)
7. *Ourselves*	Nah.

The only blameless "suspect" is God. He is *always* good both in His character and to His children. Saying "I can't help it; this is just how God made me" when we're snippy, judgmental, or unloving is a cop-out. Our heavenly Father did not design His daughters to stomp through life irritated and impatient, to cut down people with criticism and conditional love, or to sacrifice our health for half-baked projects that won't last anyway.[20]

As for the other six "suspects," there's plenty of blame to go around. And around. And around. And around. But staying on the guilt-go-round means we're moving every direction except forward, and it's forward that I believe God wants us to go. Not in pride in or shame of our Marthaness, but in an enlightened dependence upon Him—and the shoes of our choice.

---

* The latest method, approved by church boards worldwide, is sitting on a wooden pew and listening to the arthritic stylings of organist Melva Schwaplingel play "Brighten the Corner Where You Are" for two hours straight or until she gets it right, whichever comes first.

CHAPTER EIGHT

The Worst Sin

There are some things this world would be better off without.

I started a list, but the more it grew, the more agitated I became. Chest pains forced me to stop at 9,842 (commercials for podiatrists that air during the dinner hour, complete with colorful graphics of bunions). Let's just cut to the chase: The worst sin is leisure suits.

If you're too young to remember leisure suits, watch reruns of *The Brady Bunch* and *Starsky and Hutch*. (See the thick, stifling fabrics? See the wide lapels? See the long, pointy collars? These were worn by stunt doubles. The real actors lounged in their trailers in flannel pajamas.) *The Lawrence Welk Show* alone, which costumed its cast in miles of psychedelic polyester, is responsible for the prickly heat rash of untold millions who merely wanted to look "wunnerful".

The only thing worse than seeing a man in a leisure suit was seeing him wear it with a *tie*. If a thousand years from now, archaeologists dig up a time capsule and find a polyester leisure suit, they will rightly conclude it was an instrument of torture.

Besides, isn't *leisure suit* an oxymoron? If it's designed for men who are unable to differentiate between work and play, then the only vocation it's fit for is lounge lizard. (Gold medallions and fake chest hair sold separately.)

My pulse is starting to race. Maybe we should talk instead about what's on your hit list. Maybe you like polyester leisure suits, but can't stand plastic pink flamingos. Maybe you like gaudy yard art, but can't stand polka music. Maybe you like to roll out the barrel, but can't stand a lot of sentences beginning with the word *maybe*.

Trying to agree on the world's worst sin is pointless. It's like debating how many choir directors can dance on the head of a pin, which has resulted in more church splits than you can shake a hymnal at.* Instead of debating which is worst, let's talk about which was first. What do you think was the first sin?

1. The appealing yet deceptive infomercial that Satan produced to tempt Eve. ("Act now and receive a lifetime supply of remorse—*absolutely free!*")
2. Adam and Eve eating the forbidden fruit without first washing their hands.
3. Lucifer rebelling against God before the world was created.

If you're thinking *apple,* forget it. The first sin wasn't committed in a garden by a human, but in heaven by an angel.

Sin, as we know, is anything less than absolute holiness. It seems to me that violent rebellion against the Almighty falls into that category. Ergo, the first falling short of God's holiness was Lucifer's aspiration to ascend higher than the Highest.

---

* Second only to the top church-splitting issue, "Does toe tapping count as dancing?"

THAT FIRST SIN IS A DOOZY

Every star has a name, but angels are without number. Scripture identifies at least three, though: Gabriel (who announced the conceptions of John the Baptist and Jesus), Michael (a battling archangel), and Lucifer (flashy dresser and musician).[1] Don't believe me? Read God's soliloquy about the most infamous of fallen angels.

> You were in Eden,
> the garden of God;
> every precious stone adorned you:
> ruby, topaz and emerald,
> chrysolite, onyx and jasper,
> sapphire, turquoise and beryl.
> Your settings and mountings were made of gold. . . .
>
> All your pomp has been brought down to the grave,
> along with the noise of your harps. . . .[2]

Lucifer, whose name means "light bearer," may have been a glittering guardian cherub on the outside. But on the inside, he was an insolent sycophant thinking "phooey, phooey, phooey" instead of "holy, holy, holy." Eventually, he spoke the words that altered heaven and earth forever: "I will be like the Most High."[3] That detonated a holy war, with every angel choosing sides. When the celestial combat ended, the angels in the white hats had won. Lucifer and his cronies have been in payback mode ever since.

Here's where it gets really interesting for us Marthas. When Lucifer said, "I will be like the Most High," he didn't just commit the first recorded offense against God. He became the first perfectionist.

★   ★   ★

Mercy sakes. I didn't think perfectionism was *that* bad, but then I guess I never thought about from whence it came.

Still, if we agree that a perfectionist is someone who wants perfection, then Lucifer qualifies as the first one. Perfection, with all its power and glory, is precisely what he craved most. He saw it

firsthand, too. Authentic, immaculate, glorious, pure perfection—
and every bit of it was God's alone.

Scripture doesn't give us any time markers for eternity past, so
we don't know how many minutes (or millennia) Lucifer waited
until he rebelled. But he observed perfection long enough to
know this: It couldn't be stolen. It couldn't be created. But it could
be faked.

PERCEPTION IS NINE-TENTHS OF THE LIE

Counterfeits only "work" when they look like the real thing.
Try offering your bank teller a wad of twenties with Bugs Bunny's
picture on them. Then you can watch your television debut on
America's Dumbest Criminals from your jail cell. It doesn't matter if
the object is jewelry, furs, art, luggage, or aluminum siding. The
imitation has to pass for the authentic.

The trouble is, most of what we crave—believing it to be perfect
—is imperfect. Calling ourselves "imperfectionists" would be more
apt. (Maybe "per*fiction*ists"would be better still since perfection is a
fantasy.) All those things we're maxed out for—the perfect job,
perfect mate, perfect children, perfect appearance, perfect house—
are inherently and terminally imperfect.

Part of the reason we hound this illusion is because, quite simply, it looks so good! Dr. David Stoop, a psychologist, put it this
way: "The lie [of perfection] is based on the fact that when people
are faced with the choice between what is *possible* and what is *desirable,* they usually choose what is desirable, whether it is possible or
not."[4] Experience and logic tell us perfection isn't possible, yet we
still perceive it as desirable. Based on that doomed perception, nine-
tenths of which is false, we struggle along like misguided Quixotes.

Several years ago, my family was on a chips and salsa kick. We
tried various store-bought brands without success. Then, at a state
fair, I saw a demonstration booth for salsa makers. The hawker
whipped up batch after batch of fragrant, zesty salsa that made my
mouth water. Wide-eyed, I watched her toss tomatoes, peppers,
and spices into the salsa maker. She made a few expert cranks on
the handle and presto! Out came the freshest and most flavorful

salsa I have ever experienced. Her rapid patter on the salsa maker's virtues mesmerized me. Its many uses (carrot salad *and* cole slaw!). Its easy-to-clean construction (dishwasher safe!). Its ability to nourish my children with an all-natural, low-fat snack (homemade!). Its power to strengthen my marriage (aphrodisiac jalapeños!). I had to have one.

Alas, my salsa making was a total flop. Never mind trying to hit upon the right combination of ingredients in my salsa maker. I couldn't even operate it! The saleswoman, with a big smile and a small twist of the wrist, had wrought world-class salsa. I had to brace one knee on the kitchen counter, grip the dumb thing in a headlock, and crank for all I was worth. The only thing I wrought was a wrenched elbow.

Average salsa was possible, but perfect salsa was desirable. That's what I went for, and I ended up with none.

GO EAST, YOUNG MARTHA! GO EAST!

We perfectionistic Marthas like to think of ourselves as intelligent women. Sharp. Savvy. Perceptive. We like to think of ourselves as independent women, too. Free. Aloof. Self-reliant. We're a double threat, with the whip of authority in one hand and the reins of control in the other. Look out, world, it's Marthas ho! We're eating up the prairie, breaking new ground, and forging new frontiers. Sort of like Rambo in calico.

But if we'd stop long enough for a good look over our shoulders, we wouldn't see the competition eating our dust as we might suppose they are. We'd see the grim figure of Perfectionism hunched in the driver's seat with a whip in one hand and the reins in the other. The heavy harness is on *our* backs. Here's my question, then: *If we're so liberated and smart, why are we in bondage to a lie?*

Because we've been deceived.

Did you know there are more verses in the New Testament warning us against deception than against temptation? This is because much of our behavior results from our thoughts. Lucifer didn't one day command Eve, "Sin!" and she said, "Okey-dokey!" She had to be deceived.[5]

Before you puff up in a defensive I'm-way-too-smart-to-be-deceived posture, think of this. Eve had never sinned, and yet she was deceived. Eve lived in a perfect world with only one other person (who also happened to be perfect), and yet she was deceived. Eve had no career or domestic demands to distract her, and yet she was deceived. Eve had no emotional baggage, and yet (you guessed it) she was deceived. Eve walked and talked with God Himself every evening, and yet (say it with me) she was deceived. Eve had only one possible temptation, and yet (take it on home) she was deceived.

How different from you and me! We were born with sin natures. We live in a deteriorating world with billions of imperfect people. We don't have daily chats with God in His physical presence. We are bombarded with countless demands, issues, and temptations on every front. How, given all that, can we rightly conclude that we're immune to deception? Such a thought, in my opinion, is the best proof that we're not.

THE ANGEL FORMERLY KNOWN AS LUCIFER

Satan is described many ways in Scripture. We're going to look specifically at just three because they relate to our struggle with perfectionism. But before we get in too deep, remember this: "Greater is He who is in you than he who is in the world."[6] This is more important than using coasters, seat belts, or fabric softener—*combined.*

Father of Lies

This is one of Satan's better-known sobriquets. The first falsehood originated with him, and it begat lots of little falsehoods and so on and so on.[7] These lies are like roaches. They hate light, and if you see one skittering across your kitchen floor, you can be sure there are plenty more nearby. Here are five fundamental lies targeted to Marthas.

> *Lie #1* If we tried harder, we could get everything in our lives under control. Then life would be perfect and we would be happy.

Lie #2 All those inner imperatives (the I *ought to, need to, should* messages in our minds) are true. If we achieved them, our pressure and stress would go away.

Lie #3 God's love for us fluctuates, based on our performance.

Lie #4 We should use every ability we have to the utmost at all times, even if it harms us or someone else. After all, didn't Christ suffer for us?

Lie #5 Everything is equally important and urgent.

To us maxed-out Marthas, these lies are as familiar to us as the pass code to our electronic data organizers. The time has come, however, to question the motives behind this misinformation. Is it to draw us closer to God? Shower us with love? Fill our lives with meaning and joy? No way. The motive behind these lies is to keep us in bondage—chained to stress, insomnia, insecurity, worry, and even depression. Living based on these lies keeps us plodding after the impossible, sacrificing our health, relationships, and faith on the way. We end up further from God, mired in doubt, filled with anxiety, and lacking focus.

When we're tired of the toll these lies are taking on our lives, there's a way out. The secret weapon to set us free is the industrial-strength, fumigating force of *truth!* Lots of people, even those who scorn the Bible, easily quote Jesus' words, "The truth will set you free." What they often leave out is the first part: "If you hold to my teaching, you are really my disciples. *Then* you will know the truth, and the truth will set you free" (italics added).[8] We must think on, stand up for, hold on to, and move forward in truth! The next time a lie like those above pops up, let's squish it with one of the truths below.

1. Perfection is an illusion.
2. Truth sets us free; lies keep us in bondage.
3. God's love for us is based on His character, not our performance.

4. Our abilities are gifts from God to be used within healthful boundaries.
5. Only one thing is needful.

The Accuser

This nom de plume[9] reminds me of a kid who lived down the road from my childhood home. Kevin didn't like to play, though. He liked to tattle. And most of the stuff he went running to his mommy about wasn't true anyway.*

Most accusations have words like *you ought to, you need to, you should.* Or, for variety's sake, "you should *not* have, did *not* need to, ought *not* to have." If that sounds familiar, flip back a page and notice Lie #2.

Still, an accusation may or may not be a lie. In either case, you and I are on the winning side. If the accusation is true, we can confess it, receive forgiveness, and start over. If the accusation is a lie, we can zap it with truth and keep going.

Accusations only keep us in bondage to perfectionism if we do neither.

OK. So now we have two options. How can we tell which one we need to choose?

Consider how the accusation is phrased. If it's worded so that its aim is to heal, it's probably true. If it's worded so that its aim is to hurt, it's probably a lie.

Here's an example:

True accusation: Yelling at your family wasn't the best choice.
True response: Ask your kids and God for forgiveness, receive it, and start over.

False accusation: You yelled at your family, so you're a terrible person from this day forth and yea, forevermore.

---

* For instance, mixing dirt, sand, water, glue, syrup, and eggs in a big hole does *not* make real quicksand. If Kevin had stuck around longer, he would've seen that after his brother and mine pushed me in, I only sank to the top of my knee-socks. Ha! What a loser!

True response: Recall the forgiveness that is already ours, separate the offense from our identity, and keep going.

The key word in that last response is *identity*. If we choose to nurture our identity in Christ, flaming accusations fizzle into duds.

One of the best things I've read about our identity is from Neil Anderson, the founder of Freedom in Christ Ministries. (He thinks the connection between knowing our identity in Christ and being free is so vital, he based an entire ministry on it!) You can read his "Who I Am in Christ" list in chapter 18, "Resources." Sitting at Jesus' feet is good, but embracing our identity in Him is the best. For now, take glad tidings of comfort and joy that you, as a Christian, are *accepted, secure,* and *significant* in Christ.

The Destroyer

One of the most stressful events any woman endures is being professionally photographed.

You know the routine. Obsessing over what to wear. Fussing with hairstyles, makeup, and accessories. Going out the door, and then *whoosh!* A hot blast of humid air swirls around you. The naturally straight hair you coaxed into soft curls suddenly droops. Or, the naturally curly hair you tamed into a sleek "do" abruptly frizzes. The outside force over which you had no control torpedoed you big time.

The solution? Since no woman in our generation will stoop to tying a head scarf under her chin like our grandmothers did, we either need to find a photographer who makes house calls or do our grooming at the studio.

Finding a solution to the legacy of damage left by the first perfectionist is slightly more difficult. Satan is called *destroyer* in both the Old and New Testaments,[10] and like most nicknames, it's an earned one. Everything about perfectionism tears down instead of builds up. *Everything.*

It destroys our bodies as we push them beyond healthy boundaries. It destroys our relationships as we neglect them for the sake of projects. It destroys our focus by fragmenting our attention into zillions of ineffectual *ought to's*. It destroys our faith by fixating on externals. It destroys our perceived identity as we base it on performing instead of on Christ.

With fallout like this, perfectionism earns a double designation: the first sin *and* the worst sin!

All perfectionism can offer us are cheap consolation prizes. A leisure suit (lime green). A plastic pink flamingo (hail damaged, missing one eye). A collection of polka music (on eight-track tapes). Since all these things clash with my lava lamp, I'm choosing the grand prize—truth! If you're not totally convinced to choose the same, I'll throw in a pair of fuzzy dice for the rearview mirror of your car. Then you can cruise to freedom in style.

CHAPTER NINE

Keeping Up Appearances

Saturday.

A day to sleep in. Kick back. Relax. Stay in your jammies until noon. A day to clutter the living room with newspapers, empty coffee cups, and sticky cereal bowls. So what if the kids watch cartoons for hours? Your entire family deserves at least one morning a week that they don't have to rise early and rush out the door.

Ah . . . now the kids are making cookies in the kitchen. You're so tired, you can't summon the strength to holler at them not to make a mess. Besides, they sound so excited as they whisper about "surprising Mommy and Daddy." Speaking of whom, your unshaven husband putters in his baggy T-shirt and shorts with man stuff in the basement. It's probably something combustible that he has not read the directions for, but as long as you're left alone, you don't care.

Mmm . . . you'd almost forgotten how good it feels to rest; to let the details go and surrender to the chaos. The remote control is in your hand, and you've just found one of your favorite old movies starting on television. The tension is ebbing away minute by minute. In the distant ragged edges of your spirit, a restorative calm begins to seep in. Life is good.

Uh-oh . . . the telephone rings.

Before you can say, "Let the answering machine get it," your youngest child picks up the phone. Reluctant to leave your cozy corner on the couch, you listen to the one-sided conversation and pray that it's a grandma on the other end.

"HELLO!

"WHAT!

"YEAH!

"FINE!

"WHAT?

"YEAH!

"BYE!"

Warning: The story now takes a violent turn and I confess that it's my family I'm writing about. If you suffer from a weak stomach, heart, or knees, do not read the rest of this chapter unless first cleared by your physician.

AND THEN THE WHEELS FELL OFF

"Andrew!" I called into the kitchen, where he had resumed sifting flour with happy abandon. "Who was that on the phone? Was it Grandma or Mimi?"

"No. Sissa says I can't use rainbow sprinkles. Tell her I want rainbow sprinkles."

"UG!" I groaned in disgust. Apparently the only way to get an answer was to fling off my soft blanket, flee my warm spot, trudge into the kitchen, and miss part of my favorite movie. Life is hard. "Tell me who you talked to and what that person said. Was it a man?"

"No. It was a lady. Sissa says I have to use the yucky cookie sheet. Tell her I want the shiny one."

"Mom!" Elizabeth interjected, "this little twerp is driving me crazy. I'm trying to help him, but all he does is argue with me. He's making a big mess and not doing anything *right.*"

Mercy sakes. It's one thing to see yourself turn into your mother. It's another to see your daughter turning into you. But that issue will have to wait. Again I asked who was on the phone.

In a heavy, cookie-dough accent, Andrew said, "Ith wath a lady who thez theeze on huh way."

I gripped his shoulders and stared into his eyes, trying to keep the panic out of my voice and bruises off his arms. "On her way where? Here?"

"Yeth."

"This is very important, Andrew. Who did the lady say she was?"

"I don' 'member."

Elizabeth took a break from adding food coloring to the chocolate chip cookie dough.

"Andrew, tell Mom who was on the phone. Was it someone you know? A lady from church? One of our neighbors?"

Four-year-old boys, and yes, even grown men, who know they have a prized piece of crucial information will, when aggressively confronted by one or more females, become temporarily deaf, mute, or amnesiac. This is caused by a gene carried only by the male of our species as a defense mechanism. Not only does it buy time while they consider the possible repercussions of giving various answers, including one that might actually be the truth, it also puts them temporarily in control of the situation.

Marthas are expert at wresting control from others, so I deftly maneuvered Andrew out of the conversation entirely. Releasing him and turning to Elizabeth, I said, "Maybe it was Mimi after all."

"No, I think it must have been Lynn," she replied, catching my strategy at once.

"But he knows Lynn's voice. Maybe it was—"

"IT WATH A LADY NAMED ANGELA!" my son yelled, spraying rainbow sprinkles in my ear.

"Angela!" My heart skipped a beat, then kicked into overdrive. "NEAL!" My husband, hearing the alarm in my voice, raced up the basement stairs into our kitchen.

"Who's hurt?" he wheezed.

"Nobody yet, but Angela is on her way over. Andrew took the call, and I don't know how to get in touch with her to stop her!"

A good man to have in emergencies, Neal punched those magic numbers on the phone that dial back the person who just called. The voice on the other end said that Angela, who was in town for a meeting, had just left but planned to make several stops before reaching our house. We had maybe an hour to prepare for a surprise visit from one of the most intimidating people I knew.

My path and Angela's seldom crossed, but when they did, I always felt bushwhacked. If I served her cake, she would inform me between token nibbles about the chemical additives in the frosting. If I mentioned a mutual acquaintance, she would begin ticking off a list of that person's inadequacies under the guise of "prayer requests." If I praised my children's accomplishments in front of her, she would piously remind me that the only crown we should strive for is a heavenly one. I felt like saying, "I've got a crown for you, sister, and you don't have to wait for heaven to get it!"

And now she was on her way to my house.

★   ★   ★

The truth about my Saturday lifestyle might set Angela free, but it would feel like a prison sentence to me—henceforth doomed to be viewed by her as pathetically imperfect, as someone who tried to get her act together, but couldn't quite manage it.

Here's an inside look at my thoughts during that crucial moment.

Thought #1: "It's my body's fault for being tired and letting me down. I knew I should've stayed up all night cleaning just in case we had surprise company. That's the last time I'll relax on a weekend!"

Thought #2: "It's Angela's fault for being a judgmental, inconsiderate snob. She'll show up looking her best but hoping to catch me at my worst, just so she can feel superior."

Thought #3: "It's the kids' fault for messing up my kitchen . . . my house . . . my life!"

Thought #4: "It's my husband's fault for being born smart, handsome, and loving instead of rich, wealthy, and loaded. Otherwise, I could afford a professional decorator and a live-in maid."

Thought #5: "It's all God's fault for saddling me with these burdens that keep me from achieving a perfect life."

Thought #6: "Was that thunder I just heard?"

MAN YOUR BATTLE STATIONS

We Marthas often shine best during crises. When others fret and wring their hands, we size up the situation, form a battle plan, and start barking orders. Surprise inspections bring out the beast in us.

To first child: "*You* collect the dirty dishes and clean up this kitchen."

To second child. "*You* gather up those newspapers and take the trash outside. But change out of your Spiderman pajamas first."

To husband: "Run to the grocery store for expensive all-natural cookies and gourmet coffee." (Noticing his squinty-eyed glare, I added: "Please? Pretty please?")

To self while hauling out the vacuum cleaner: "It's great to be back in control."

Control? Control of what? *Control of my image.* For just a minute there, my self-proclaimed image as domestic dynamo hung in the balance. By whipping myself and my family into frenzied activity I accomplished the following:

1. I forfeited a much-needed relaxing Saturday and stole the same from my family.
2. I communicated to my family that the way we are just isn't good enough.
3. I sent the message that acceptance is based on appearances.
4. I implied that we live one way in private and another in public.

I didn't need to hear thunder again.

CREATING OUR OWN IMAGE

This drive we Marthas have to keep up appearances isn't limited to our homes. We can also obsess about how we are perceived in our careers and churches. (See how multitalented we are?) I asked my friend Charlene, who is vice president of a megacorporation, if she thinks career women must maintain the appearance of total competence, or if it's OK to admit weakness or imperfection at work.

> A professional female won't say, "I can't get all this done and I need help." The boss would only reply, "There's nothing in the budget to get help, so either get it done or I'll find someone who can." My age, fifty, is a big factor. I know they could find someone to replace me, to work more hours for less money. There are no bonus points for honesty.

Then I asked Shawnee, who is a pastor's wife and thus a walking target for being evaluated by everyone from the church mice up, how she deals with the appearance trap.

> I sometimes wonder if I have a right to be a pastor's wife. How can I lead the women of our congregation when it's taking everything I've got to hold myself together? How can I be a role model for women who have been Christians for longer than I've been alive? . . . In some unguarded corner of my mind I carry a standard: June Cleaver meets Shirley Dobson.

Certainly there's nothing wrong with wanting to show up at work, church, social events, and other public arenas looking well-groomed and being prepared to handle reasonable expectations and duties. But like the other areas of life in which Marthas obsess, what's "good enough" for everyone else is totally unacceptable for us. You might be surprised at how many millions of people think just showing up clothed and in your right mind is good enough. (In fact, law enforcement officials are strongly against anything less.)

Let's stay honest here. We maxed-out Marthas do like to put

on a good show. There's a feeling of drama and power, fueled by a competitive spirit, as we approach tasks. When we teach a class, the students can be assured that we will be expert instructors. When we host a social event, the guests can count on hospitality suitable for a sultan. When we land an assignment at work, our boss never doubts that we'll meet (or beat) the deadline with precise professionalism.

What these students, guests, and bosses may not know is how hard we work to make these things happen. Rather than admit our limitations and thus (we falsely think) lose status in their eyes, we will deprive ourselves of sleep, balanced meals, social interaction, regular breaks, and even a well-deserved reward afterwards. We will push ourselves to exhaustion and burnout rather than reveal our imperfection. Simple words like "I'm not prepared," "I can't handle it," or "I need help" are not in our vocabulary.

TOKEN EXPERT OPINION
FROM AN OVERDUE LIBRARY BOOK

There's a fancy-schmancy name for this drive we Marthas have for keeping up the appearance of perfection at all costs. I read about it in a book whose title I found irresistible: *The Perfectionist Predicament: How to Stop Driving Yourself and Others Crazy.* (Wow! Apparently perfectionism's exclusive double-action makes it one of the more efficient personality disorders. Not only can you irritate and disappoint yourself, you can *simultaneously* annoy those around you. This timesaving feature makes it better than being merely schizophrenic or paranoid. Now we perfectionists can honestly and proudly say that of all the possible personality disorders, ours is the best!)

> You may be plagued by a deep and abiding sense that you are an imposter, a fraud. Through your superhuman efforts to achieve, improve your appearance, or otherwise attain perfection, you have managed to fool plenty of people thus far. But you could be "found out" at any moment, and the prospect terrifies you. With every failure, error, or loss you run the risk that other people will see you the way you

see yourself, be bitterly disappointed or thoroughly disgusted, and end up hating, rejecting, firing, or abandoning you.

To prevent such a calamity, you devote a great deal of time and energy to what experts in the field of addictions call *impression management*. You'll go to any lengths to look good, to appear confident and knowledgeable, or to accommodate people whose love or acceptance is important to you.[1]

"Hey!" you may say as I did when I first read that, shifting into denial as naturally as a cat lands on its feet. "I'm not *that* bad!" The authors have anticipated our defensiveness.

If you are a perfectionist, you are invariably an impression manager as well. You simply cannot risk losing other people's approval, acceptance, or admiration, which you use as a substitute for self-acceptance, self-approval, and self-esteem. Lacking an internal sense of your own value, you use other people's opinions of you and other external rewards as a yardstick for measuring your worth [italics added].[2]

Though the terminology may be shiny and new, the problem itself is older than dirt.

Remember how Adam and Eve hid from God, lest He see their imperfection? Remember how Ananias and Sapphira lied for the sake of appearances? Remember how Jesus angrily rebuked those who intentionally projected a false image of themselves?[3]

His word for impression management was *hypocrisy.*

HELP! I'M TRAPPED AND I CAN'T GET OUT!

Martha of Bethany probably wanted to present an image of herself to Jesus as an exceptional hostess. But things and people kept getting in her way and out of her control. She could not manage her impression! The result? Impatience. Anger. Accusations. Not exactly qualities to put guests at ease. (Or, as in my case, qualities to endear oneself to one's family.)

Even if we can create an image of ourselves that blows the competition out of the water and rains compliments down on our ever-swelling heads, we become caught in a trap—the appearance trap. The false image we've created must then be maintained in the present and exceeded in the future. That only means *more* work and *more* stress. Is that what we really want?

One thing will open the appearance trap and set us free: truth.

Now don't worry—I'm not suggesting that we spill our inadequate guts from every pulpit in the land. I am suggesting that, with God's help, we restrain our natural Martha tendencies to think in extremes. Instead of thinking the lie, "I must always present a flawless appearance to others at all costs," we should remember the truth, "Because God's love for me is based on His character and not my performance, I will do my best at this project within healthful boundaries and then let it go."

Abandoning the lie and adopting the truth has a hidden bonus. Not only does it free us from the appearance trap, it also frees those around us. You know exactly what I mean if an intimidating person you felt was "above" you acted like a normal person in your presence.

Don't you love it when a speaker or celebrity good-naturedly shares her own shortcomings? On a recent televised awards program, a glamorous diva accepted her gleaming trophy. She probably spent more on her fabulously manicured toenails than I do on monthly groceries. But the wall of comparison, built on her appearance alone, came down when she shared this with backstage reporters: Her preschooler had thrown up in the limousine on the way to the program!

Nothing evens the playing field like common ground. Little disasters of daily life—bad hair days, cranky kids, jury-rigged pantyhose, and even dusty knickknacks—can bring us closer together if we'll just lay our image down and leave it there.

THE THRILLING CONCLUSION

Realizing how I had nearly blasted the stress level of myself and my family through the roof by trying to force a perfect impression for Angela's visit, I repented, recanted, and retreated. I rolled the vacuum cleaner back into the closet and asked my family to be seated together on the couch.

"I'm sorry," I said. "I did it again." They knew exactly what I meant, having witnessed this screwy behavior before, and their faces relaxed a bit. "I'm sorry that I slipped into the 'Winging Out with My Hair on Fire' mode and yelled at all of you in the process. No one's visit is worth this stress.

"Kids, go back to making cookies and we'll just let Miss Angela Fancy Pants see us 'as is.' You and your feelings are more important to me than how the house looks. Will you forgive me?"

As soon as I said that, Elizabeth and Andrew flew off the couch and tackled me to the floor with "We love yous" and bear hugs. I caught my husband's expression as he looked on. He still loved me, too.

Angela ended up being a no-show, but the day actually turned out pretty good. I learned to think twice before obsessing over appearances. Neal relaxed with me on the couch when the kids resumed cookie making. When he whispered sweet somethings in my ear, I mentally promised not to nitpick about appearances for the rest of the day. Which is why I can say to him now what I couldn't say then:

"Did you know you have rainbow sprinkles in your moustache?"

CHAPTER TEN

Anger, Fear, and Guilt: Are We Having Fun Yet?

Congratulations!

If you're reading this chapter, it must mean that (a) you have no anger, no fear, and no guilt and thus are reading this strictly for pleasure; (b) you *do* have anger, fear, and guilt, but are in serious denial; or (c) you feel angry that I mentioned this topic, but are afraid to tell me and will feel guilty if you skip this chapter.

For whatever reason, I'm glad you're sticking with me—and not just because I don't want to go down in flames alone.

THREE DEGREES OF IRRITATION

We Marthas may be all-or-nothing thinkers, but when it comes to anger, we go hog-wild and have *three* generous levels to describe it. Besides just me spilling my guts, two Martha Buddies, Lori and Deanna in particular, are going to spill theirs, too.

Level #1: Simmer
(mildly yet constantly annoyed)

Lori says, "Sometimes I'm so happy I can't stand myself, but I get into the opposite mode sometimes. I need to lose weight; my kids don't do anything right; what was I thinking when I married *him;* other people are so irritating, yadda, yadda, yadda."

For Deanna, who is as sharp as they come, having someone point out the obvious makes her simmer. "I just want to snap back with, 'Do I *look* stupid?' Simmer, simmer, simmer."

The kettles in the kitchen weren't the only things simmering whenever I used to visit restaurants. I complained about *everything.* The sticky menu, the crumbs on the seat, the incompetent wait staff. It has taken me years to train my observation skills to ignore pesky details and instead *focus, with contentment and optimism, on the people I'm with* so that we all have a more enjoyable time together.*

Level #2: Tempest in a Teapot
(furious inside, but can't let it show)

For Deanna, a high school teacher, the tempest comes when she is blamed for others' failure, "*Especially students and their parents!* I had a parent call me this week, upset that her son had made a D and that I hadn't called her about his grade. This is the same parent that I've talked to on numerous occasions about her son's grade and why he was doing poorly. Yet somehow I'm the one responsible for his making a D. I just boil inside while being Miss Diplomat on the outside."

"I can identify with this one big time," says Lori. "I'm pretty good at stuffing, then I blow like that whistle on the teapot!

"I was at the high-tech photocopier yesterday copying some

---

* Although it still really bugs me when I *specifically ask* for the nonsmoking area and the host seats me *right next to* the smoking section where the only thing between me and the Marlboro Man is a six-inch high row of dusty plastic plants, one leaf of which has a glob of maple syrup on it that is slowly dripping onto my dry-clean only blouse. (Deep cleansing breath, Debi, and let it go, just let it go . . . to Level #2, that is.)

homeschool pages in triplicate for my kids. Well, the paper jammed after I had completely entered all of the pages I needed into the copier's memory (which took me an hour) and was ready to hit that nifty button to just spit out *over three hundred pages!* So Mr. Helpful Employee comes over and hits the 'clear modes' button right off the bat and right after I asked him not to [and so] those over-three-hundred pages were wiped from the copier's memory. I made it clear what he had done and I don't think he even understood. He was kind of like, 'Well, duh, sorry.' I guess you could categorize that as 'Tempest in a Teapot.' It was close to the next category, but because I didn't actually put my hands around Mr. Helpful's neck, slowly squeezing the life out of his body, it should stay in this category. I felt like crying. When I look back . . . all about paper! Pretty silly, huh?"

No, Lori. I don't think it's silly at all. What would be silly would be not writing down that whippersnapper's name and calling corporate headquarters as soon as you got home.

Level #3: Winging Out with My Hair on Fire
(overreacting, feeling surrounded by idiots, stomping, and griping)

Lori says, "I feel this, but because of my great stuffing ability, I don't explode too often. When I do, it's usually accompanied by lots of tears and I just lose it emotionally."

Ditto with Deanna. "I don't get here often. Just with students when they're consistently refusing to do as I ask. Then I leave the room and take deep breaths. Sometimes I cry to release that kind of anger."

There are plenty of examples of me in this third level of anger, but space (and my pride) won't allow me to include them all. I know you're deeply disappointed by this, but my frantic reaction to surprise company that you read in the previous chapter will just have to suffice.

★   ★   ★

Can you identify with any of these situations? I'm sure you can! Author and former pastor David Seamands says, "I have yet to counsel a performance-based and perfectionistic Christian who was not at heart *an angry person.* This doesn't mean that such persons are always *aware of* or *express* it openly. They often impress us as being extremely controlled or very loving."[1] (There's that impression management skill we learned about in chapter 9!)

Nicole Johnson, who with her husband Paul forms a marriage-themed Christian acting duo, says, "Anger is hard for women to admit. We're afraid because there's a stigma attached to it. Men are considered powerful when they're angry; women are called irrational or out of control. But my anger shouldn't have come as a surprise. It had been staring me in the face. I just didn't want to own it."[2]

Both Lori and Deanna are aware of the anger in their lives, and each has an insight on dealing with it. When I asked, "What's the number one thing that would lessen your struggle with anger?" Lori replied, "Loving like Jesus." Deanna said, "Remembering that no matter what I'm going through, especially when I'm wronged, it isn't the Cross."

While it's not a sin to reach our limit of tolerance, what we do when we get there can be. Scripture says that prior to our spiritual rebirth and transformation through Christ, we were "by nature children of wrath," which made us prone to "hatred, contentions . . . outbursts of wrath."[3] My grandma called these "hissy fits." My dad called it "going around on your high horse." Whatever—they are not the result of Spirit-filled living!

WHISTLING IN THE DARK

We may not like to admit it, but we Marthas are, at heart, great big fraidycats. Not sure you agree? Try this little test. On a scale of 1 to 5, rate how you would feel in the following scenarios, with 1 being fearless and 5 being petrified.

1. Eating my favorite kind of doughnut—after accidentally dropping it on the bakery floor.

   1   2   3   4   5

2. Going to the store to buy fifteen matching shoe storage containers to complete a closet reorganization project—and finding only fourteen.

   1   2   3   4   5

3. Being called upon to speak in public—with little or no time to prepare, let alone photocopy handouts, gather door prizes, and make 125 table favors to coordinate with my outfit.

   1   2   3   4   5

4. Inviting four people to my house for a formal dinner—and opening the door to welcome six.

   1   2   3   4   5

5. Writing a quiz in a book—and then having no mathematical skills by which to come up with an accurate scoring system.

   1   2   3   4   5

Hey, I'm a writer, not an accountant. Let's just say that if you had a lot of fours and fives, you're on the fearful side.

Most of our fears are control based. When things happen beyond our control, we are *not* happy campers. For example, visits from her in-laws send Lori into a tailspin—especially if they're spontaneous.

Allow me to quote from yet another overdue library book: "Many obsessives have a *disproportionate* need for control—one that is driven and rigid, rather than reasonable and flexible. This exaggerated need stems from an irrational conviction that perfect control can ensure safe passage through life."[4] Safe passage. That's it! A safe passage means a perfect life. The problem is, life is full of hazards. *People* that don't think or do the way we believe they should. *Events* that don't go the way we planned. *Dentists* who play Muzak way too loud, as if we won't notice that they're drilling clear through to our spines.

When it comes to our spiritual life, surrendering control often ends up like a Holy Spirit-hokey pokey. We Marthas put a little bit in, take a little bit out. Instead of yielding every bit of ourselves once and for all, we offer tentative dabs on a trial basis. If God handles that OK, we might offer a tad more next time. Bill Hybels, pastor of Willow Creek Community Church, spoke to me and others who feel this way.

> They fear [Jesus] wants to break into their lives and rob them of the joy of living. They are sure he wants to limit their freedom and make them live in confinement. . . . Sometimes these people come to me and say, "I sense that God wants greater control of my life, and I don't want to let him in. I'm fighting him."
>
> I usually tell them, "Don't worry—you'll win. You can keep God out. Slam the door, put bars on the windows and close your mind. You can stop him." But I also tell them that they don't understand who Jesus is. He is not a thief, but an anti-thief. He knocks patiently until you open the door, and then he fills up your house with a whole truckload of life's most precious commodities.
>
> Christ is an altruistic lover: he loves us for what he can give us, not for what he can get from us. If you tear down the bars on the windows, unbolt your doors and fling them wide open so that he can come in, he will fill your house with everything it needs in order to be warm, and beautiful and pleasant to live in.[5]

Wow. A warm, beautiful, and pleasant place to live sounds good to me! Make it self-cleaning as well, and then even in-law-phobic Lori would be satisfied.

I'VE GOT GUILT LIKE A RIVER

Our temperaments often have a wide streak of the conscientious personality style in them. This is why, for example, we always return extra change, shopping carts, and library books. Well, *some* of us return library books. I show my conscientiousness in other ways. For example, whenever a police helicopter circles my neighborhood I fight the compulsion to run outside screaming, "It was me! I did it! I'm the one who thoughtlessly forgot to use my turn signal on the freeway yesterday when I changed lanes!"

This extreme sensitivity had no off button. Every time a need presented itself, my first reaction was "I *ought to* help. I *need to* get involved. I *should* do that. After all, I'm a *Christian!*" It didn't matter what it was—taking cookies to a new neighbor or feeding the starving masses of the entire planet.

Finally, I had to release the care of the world to God. Once I had determined my life's focus (which I'll explain more in chapter 17), I was free to turn down or even turn away from heart-wrenching needs without being consumed with guilt.

Remember that not even Jesus Himself healed every person or righted every wrong during His earthly life. Why, then, do we think we should? Are we mightier than God? Does He expect us to say yes to absolutely everything? No on both counts. Too often we believe that unless we are exhausted to the point of collapse and guilt-ridden to the point of despair, we're not truly "living sacrifices" for God. Seems to me, though, that during the era in which actual sacrifices were made to atone for sin, God required those without blemish of any kind.[6] Offering God a weak and wobbly lamb displeased Him. When we overcommit and overwork because we have no idea what our purpose, or focus is, we become weak and wobbly in both body and spirit. Keeping our focus on the specific things God has both called and gifted us to do is an essential key to freedom from the maxed-out lifestyle. It's also integral to the "one thing" Jesus spoke of.

Lori says she felt the same way about focus. "I went through this big-time last year. How freeing it was to realize God wanted me just to focus on our homeschooling and family at this time. When we get into so many things, we miss out on the joy of the very thing God has called us to. I have a hard time keeping the proper focus when I am trying to do it all."

Having focus helps Deanna keep guilt at bay, too. "With the endless 'sign-up to help' lists that go around my Sunday school class, I don't sign up unless it is related directly to an outreach ministry at low-income apartments where I serve each week. I've narrowed my focus and have said no continually to being a youth sponsor, to leading a Bible study, to working in the nursery, etc. Just sticking with what 'lights my fire' and saying no to most everything else has freed me lots."

Guilt is not a bad thing to be avoided. No, a bad thing to be avoided would be trusting your hair to a bargain beautician whose earrings are little plastic troll dolls. (Don't even *ask* me how I know this.) Instead, guilt is a neutral thing to be evaluated. Is it true guilt? If so, it will point out a specific way we missed the mark somewhere. We deal with this by asking for *and accepting* forgiveness through Christ. Is it false guilt? If so, it will nag about vague failures everywhere. We deal with this by reaffirming our identity in Christ.

CHRISTIAN WOMEN
GET THE DOUBLE WHAMMY

One of the biggest factors in the current maxed-out lifestyles of Marthas is the feminist movement. Thanks to it, we women can open our own doors, pay for our own meals, and give men our seat in the last lifeboat. The problem for us overly conscientious types, though, is that we have distorted the message that *women can be anything* into the mandate that *we should do everything.*

Secular voices tell us we need whiter teeth, faster cars, softer hair, bigger houses, and cleaner kids. Couple this sky-high societal goal with lofty standards for faith, and *shazam!* We've been hit by the Double Whammy! Listen to Jean Fleming, author of *Finding Focus in a Whirlwind World.*

In the twenty years I've been a Christian, I've received instruction on and been challenged to read my Bible daily, pray without ceasing, do in-depth Bible study regularly, memorize Scripture, meditate day and night, fellowship with other believers, always be ready to give an answer to the questioning unbeliever, give to missions and to the poor, work as unto the Lord, use my time judiciously, give thanks in all circumstances, serve the Body using my gifts to edify others, keep a clean house as a testimony, practice gracious hospitality, submit to my husband, love and train my children, disciple other women, manage finances as a good steward, involve myself in school and community activities, develop and maintain non-Christian friendships, stimulate my mind with careful reading, improve my health through diet and exercise, color coordinate my wardrobe, watch my posture, and "simplify" my life by baking my own bread.[7]

Another woman expresses the Double Whammy as hitting us so hard that we splinter into what she calls the "Fractured Christian Woman." Here's part of Peg Rankin's description of the FCW philosophy.

1. Take on more than you can handle. You can never do enough for God.
2. Try to be all things to all people. That's how you show God's love.
3. Set goals and push yourself to achieve them. You want to hear "well done" on Judgment Day.
4. Rarely take time off. There's too much work to be done. You're expected to burn out for God.
5. Keep on pouring out, even when there's little left to give. The Christian life is not for quitters.
6. Be willing to sacrifice everything for your ministry: your family, your friends, even your health. These things are temporal; kingdom work is eternal.
7. Think twice about saying no to a Christian opportunity. If you do, feel guilty, *really* guilty.[8]

Enough already! The Double Whammy is too much to bear. Not only do these descriptions inspire more guilt, but also more fear, more anger, and more talks with my travel agent about a one-way ticket to Denial.

OUT OF CONTROL

Life is full of ironies.

We can go for weeks without spilling anything on the kitchen floor. But the day we supershine it is the day we'll drop an entire carton of eggs.

We usually appear in public well-groomed. But the one time we decide to dash to the post office "as is," we run into an old high school chum who then spreads the word on how we've gone downhill.

We can set our VCRs to tape-record the final installment of a riveting *Masterpiece Theatre* series. Viewing it the next day, we find that because of the public television station's fund-raising pleas, the last twenty minutes of the actual show are missing.

There is one instance, though, when irony works for us: when we control-freaks yield control. Here's how it has worked for me.

My anger is reduced when I release others from their mistakes.

My fear is reduced when I release worry about all the "what-ifs."

My guilt is reduced when I release myself from my mistakes.

Thanks to God's grace, I'm not the maxed-out woman I was fifteen years ago. Just thinking of the freedom I have today makes me feel like celebrating! Let's meet at the Whistlestop for cheesecake. If the Marlboro Man's there, I'll even send a slice over to him with my compliments.

CHAPTER ELEVEN

Martha Moms: The Perils of Perfectionistic Parenting

Back in the 1960s, my mom, Beth, and her friend "Millie" decided to swap the household chores they hated most. Beth hated ironing clothes, and Millie hated cleaning her kitchen. They struck the deal over a tall, icy bottle of Royal Crown cola, and my mom faithfully showed up at Millie's the next week with a basket of ironing.

Millie, showing herself to be a true woman of foresight, hadn't lifted a finger in her kitchen since striking the barter seven days before. Seven *long* days before with three meals in each and plenty of snacking. Millie's four growing boys ate constantly and soon every dish, plate, and utensil was soiled. Enterprising Millie turned her Melamine upside down and the brood ate off the back side of the plates. (Really!) Every inch of the kitchen was covered in sticky messes, gloppy dishes, sour linens, and smelly trash. The cats loved it. They swaggered among the food-encrusted debris on the dining table like smug Cleopatras through piles of gold.

"Oh, good! You're here!" cried Millie. She grabbed Beth's basket and scurried off to watch her soap operas while she ironed. My mom, who is way too nice to call someone a "lazy, dipstick, homemaker pig" to her face, cleaned that entire kitchen. To be fair, Millie did a beautiful job of ironing. To be honest, that was the first and last time they traded chores.

We may now describe Millie's household management technique as "survival of the fittest." A little more than a year after this fiasco, Millie gave birth to another son and, when a family emergency arose, she needed someone to care for little Donald.

"Of course I'd be glad to help you," Beth said over the phone. "Do you have any idea how long—? Hang on a minute. Someone's at the door."

There stood Millie with babe in arms. She arrived so quickly because she traveled light—all she packed was the baby. No clothes. No diapers. No bottles. No toys. Considering Millie's expertise with all things domestic, my mom was just thankful she showed up with Donny and not one of the cats stuffed into a little sailor suit.

Donny flourished under my mother's care. She cleared up the angry-red rash on his bottom with an innovative treatment Millie had never considered: regular diaper changes. Mom further let Donny have his first taste of pure milk from sanitized bottles. He much preferred this to the "it's not cheese yet" formula Millie used. My older brother's baby clothes fit Donny, and although they were hand-me-downs, they were always matched, mended, and clean.

A few weeks later, another of my mom's friends called to see how the baby-sitting-turned-adoption was progressing.

"Any word yet from Millie on when she plans to get him back?" Justine asked.

"No," Beth replied. "But I'm not in a hurry. Donny's so sweet. He hardly ever fusses, even though he's picked up a cold. I don't know where he got it, though, because none of us are sick."

But Justine knew. "You washed him, didn't you?"

Apparently, bathing children from Darwinian homes removes the protective crust, thus exposing them to the bacterial hazards that foolish hygienic people like us Martha-types are constantly battling.

Millie finally claimed her son. Last we heard, he was a strapping Marine, highly decorated for valor. One story described how his entire platoon was wiped out in a filthy, disease-infested jungle camp, and yet he alone survived.

I think we all know why.

RUB-A-DUB . . . NOT

One of the ironies of parenting is that though we may be bewildered at our own child-rearing problems, we are expert at solving everyone else's. My mom thought Donny needed a sparkling clean home, but God knew better.

And that's the rub. *God knew better.* Too often, we Marthas think we know best.

Do you remember how wise you were before you had kids? Me too. In true Martha form, I didn't let lack of experience stop me from criticizing. Here are just a few of my astute observations regarding my friends who married and multiplied before I did.

Problem:
   One-year-old child won't sleep through the night.
Mother's reaction:
   Comfort the child upon each awakening and reason with him on why "nighttime is for sleepy-bye."
My solution:
   Let child cry it out after purchasing military-grade ear protection.

Problem:
   Two-year-old refuses to ride in car seat.
Mother's reaction:
   Let child roam loose in car or hold on lap while driving.
My solution:
   Make citizen's arrest of child; submit own name for safety award.

Problem:
    Three-year-old has fit in store.
Mother's reaction:
    Bribe child with treats and toys.
My solution:
    Threaten to exchange child at customer service desk.*

Until a Martha *is* a full-time, sleep-deprived, sticky-furnitured, Cheerios-trailing, chronically-out-of-cash mother, she just won't have a clue about parenting. However, like I did, she probably thinks she has all the answers. When I think of the self-righteous *shoulds* I aimed at new parents, I cringe. Never fear, though, because my turn came.

CULTURE SHOCK

My pregnancy with baby number one sped by as I prepared the ultimate nursery. I sewed the curtains, quilt, and bumper pad myself. I read all the popular books on pregnancy, labor and delivery, and newborn care. I stocked up on disposable diapers, designed the birth announcements, and filled the freezer with casseroles. I was ready for motherhood.

What a joke.

Elizabeth, as precious and adorable as she was, didn't understand my plans. When I put her down for a nap, I wanted her to sleep for two hours. No more, no less. She decided to either enter a six-hour, coma-like slumber (resting up for her all-nighter) or just stay awake and fuss.

When I dressed her in the morning, I figured that was one job done for the day and we could all go on with our lives. Wrong. Elizabeth was a spitter. The dark green robe I wore back then told the tale. By midafternoon (I still hadn't had time to shower and dress), I looked like I'd been standing under a flock of pigeons, and Elizabeth had gone through about fourteen outfits.

---

* Of course, now that I have nearly twenty combined years of parenting experience, my solutions to the above problems are kinder . . . gentler . . . simpler. In a word, codeine.

Dirty laundry multiplied like rabbits. Neal and I existed on cold cereal, canned soup, and frozen pizzas. I grieved for the days when I had the time, energy, and money to prepare an entire meal from soup to nuts. I mourned for the time when I left the house each day smartly groomed and dressed for success—and all before dark, too.

In short, I wanted my mommy.

AND THE GUILT GOES ON

The realities of down and dirty parenting hit me hard. Motherhood for many of us perfectionistic, project-oriented, Type A, Martha Moms, to put it mildly, stinks. During this era, we struggle with the *highest expectations* and the *lowest productivity levels* we've ever known. Our time and energy reserves are chronically depleted. Frustration over constantly falling short of what we think we *should* be able to do intensifies. No amount of prenatal planning can ready us for the mind-bending horrors of nonstop childcare.

The culture shock experienced with the first baby is bad enough. Add to that the unique challenges of each successive child and we understand why Dr. Dobson titled one of his books *Parenting Isn't for Cowards*.

Sheryl says, "Because of the differing personalities of my children, I find I structure my parenting style to fit their needs." Less flexible Marthas find such distinctives exasperating as they attempt to micromother their kids and themselves into synchronized perfection.

Elizabeth suffered through my "new parent intensity to do everything perfectly" barrage. Feedings and naps came on schedule, not demand. A bottle dropped on the floor suffered such gross contamination that I speed-dialed the Haz-Mat* team to dispose of it. Color-coded baskets lined gleaming shelves for various types of highly educational toys. The result? She has a personality described as "a party waiting to happen."

Almost eight years later, I had Andrew. By then, my arches had fallen and so had my expectations of perfect parenting.

---

* Hazardous Materials Team. Think of them as the bomb squad of germs.

He ate when he was hungry and slept when he was sleepy. If a bottle hit the floor, I brushed it against my pants' leg before returning it to him. His toys were unceremoniously dumped in mismatched laundry baskets beneath the changing table. And yet this kid is so uptight about organization, I'm sure the alpha-helix of his DNA is straight instead of spiraled.

Though Lori says her Marthaness lessened with the birth of each of her children, she also discovered a universal truth: The tips and tricks we learned with baby number one don't always work with baby number two. Where one is reticent, the other is fearless. Where one is artistic, the other is athletic. And none of our children seems to be the slightest bit concerned with *our* mastermind ideals. Their interests lie elsewhere. Who gets the window seat; who chooses the next video; who can burp the loudest.

What's a Martha Mom to do when both she and her offspring have sprung off the perfection track? Susan Lenzkes put her advice in poem form.

I searched—

but there definitely was not

a packet of instructions

attached to my children

when they arrived.

And none has since

landed in my mailbox.

Lord, show me how

to be a good parent.

Teach me to

correct without crushing,

help without hanging on,

listen without laughing,

surround without smothering,

and love without limit—

the way You love me.[1]

THAT'S AMORÈ

One night stands out in my mind as a turning point in my understanding of God's love. As I watched Elizabeth sleeping in her crib, I felt *consumed* with love. There's no other word for it. My eyes drank in every detail, from her chubby cheeks to her tiny toes. Even the sound of her breathing filled me with an adoring kind of ache; almost as if I would burst if she became any more precious to me.*

Did I love her because of how she performed? Not at all. I loved her simply because she came from me. She belonged to me. She was mine. And that was when I knew, for the first time, that God *loved me.* I belonged to Him in Christ. I was His.

Nothing can change God's affection for us. Not productivity, not neediness, not success, not failure. That's because His love is not based on what we do and how well, but on His character, which can't *not* love His own children with a perfect, enduring, irrevocable love.

I sat on the floor in Elizabeth's darkened room, hugging my knees and unable to stop smiling. God's unconditional love finally clicked, and He used a few pounds of demanding humanity, dressed in pink pajamas, to do it.

Since that night, I've been a mom on a mission. My job is to convince my children that, because of who they are in Christ, God loves them—no matter what. My biggest obstacle in completing this mission is . . . me!

MARTHA'S VINEGAR

Another of the ironies of parenting is how mushy we feel toward our kids when they're sleeping, and how irritated we get with them when they're awake. Being a Martha Mom, I found myself getting into the "every time I look at you you're doing

---

* I felt exactly the same way when my son Andrew was born.

something wrong" habit. As my kids grew older and I became busier, it got worse—and did little to communicate unconditional love.

When they were tiny, I had (naturally) low expectations for their behavior. *Of course* toddlers are going to spill juice and scatter toys. *Of course* preschoolers are going to dress themselves weird.*

Sheryl observed that "it was easier to be a 'perfect' parent when the children were most dependent upon me. As they grow older and I have less control, I find out rather quickly my own imperfections." She's right. As Elizabeth and Andrew grew older, my tolerance went down and my expectations went up. This is an imperfection I hate to admit, but I'm willing to do it right here in front of God and everybody because I believe lots of other Martha Moms are in the same leaky boat.

Tolerance becomes tiresome when its source is not God. The natural Martha in me, notorious for shooting from the lip, can take one look at my kids and instantly fire off an inventory of infractions:

"Get your hair out of your eyes."

"Quit leaning against the wallpaper."

"Eat that in the kitchen, not the living room."

There are two Scripture verses that have helped me take the sting out of my perfectionistic perspective.

The first is James 1:20. The *New King James Version* says, "The wrath of man does not produce the righteousness of God." *The Message* translates it, "God's righteousness doesn't grow from human anger."

The second verse, speaking of the godly woman, is Proverbs 31:26. It says, "On her tongue is the law of kindness." The *New*

---

* A typical outfit for Elizabeth during her preschool "I can dress myself" stage nearly struck me blind. A neon orange T-shirt, a red plaid wool skirt, aqua tights, pink sandals, assorted gaudy jewelry from garage sales, and, secured with a sparkly headband, a dryer sheet for a veil. My solution: "Sweetheart! Weren't you creative today with your clothes! Here, before we leave the house, let's put these big 'I dressed myself today' stickers on your shirt—one on the front and one on the back." Elizabeth felt as proud of the stickers, which I made from address labels, as she did of her clothes, and I was absolved from all responsibility for her appearance. Andrew showed similar panache during his self-dressing phase, but I couldn't convince him to wear the stickers. (And he wondered why we stayed home a lot.)

Living Translation puts it, "When she speaks, her words are wise, and kindness is the rule when she gives instruction."

Put together into the familiar cross-stitched version, "You catch more flies with honey than vinegar."

When my kids are with all their cousins, there is major toy dispersion. This Martha Mom will stomp over to my kids and slosh vinegar all over the place. "All right! That's it! I've told you to get that living room cleaned up three times and you still haven't done it! Just because you're playing with your cousins doesn't mean you can trash every room in the house! Yadda, yadda, yammer, yammer, nag, nag!"

My sister-in-law, Juliana, uses honey. She calmly goes to the kids, gets down on their level, and just watches them. Then she says something like, "Tell me about your game. . . . Yeah? That's cool. . . . Listen, I think you've been having so much fun in here that you forgot about putting toys away in the living room. You probably didn't even hear me and your mom ask you to clean up. Why don't you run in there now, put your stuff away, and when you come back, I'll play this with you for a few minutes?"

It works every time. The kids obey. Peace is kept. And I receive a much-needed reminder that affirming is better than attacking.

That's not to say that affirmation overlooks basic disciplines of respect, orderliness, and responsibility. But it does say that our children's ever-fluctuating mastery of those disciplines does not affect our love for them.[2]

They've *got* to know this, but we can't give what we don't have. This is why I believe getting a grip on God's unconditional love for *us* is the best thing we can do for our kids. (Well, that and making sure they floss.)

FODDER FOR FUTURE THERAPY SESSIONS

Shawnee, intentionally childless at this writing, worries about her ability to be a good parent. "Will I pass on my perfectionism to [my kids] so that they can't accept the way God made them? Will *I* accept the way God made them? The forming of a soul is a terrifying prospect."

Terrifying, indeed.

The four perils we've seen in this chapter alone are enough to make any woman volunteer for a Peace Corps posting to Antartica. By way of review, those perils are:

1. Know-it-all thinking before we have children ourselves;
2. Culture shock when we have our first baby;
3. Derailment from the perfection track;
4. Our tendency to overcorrect and underaffirm.

According to counselor Dr. Chuck Lynch, perfectionistic parents *do* leave lasting marks on their children. He says, "Even when we are adults and our parents are in their older years, have mellowed out and become more accepting and caring, [they] may not resemble what they were like in early parenting years. We are acting out now how they parented us early on."[3]

So now what? Have we Martha Moms totally blown it? Are our children doomed to expensive therapy to recover from our insistence during their youngest years that they "wash their hands and say their prayers 'cuz God and germs are everywhere"?

Dr. Lynch says the only thing worse than a mistake is an uncorrected one.*

> Perfectionistic parenting has nothing to do with the child, and everything to do with the mom because perfectionism is fear based, not faith based. It is based on the mother's fear of discovery [that she has flaws], rejection, and abandonment.
>
> Therefore, it would be important to go to the child and say, "I was wrong for XYZ. What I did, I did out of my fear, not your failure. Would you please forgive me?"[4]

Let me assure you, whenever I do this with my kids they cover me with hugs and kisses. Their forgiveness energizes me to resist perfectionism, and then we're all more happy and relaxed.

---

* No kidding! Don't you hate misshelved items in a store? I can't pass by the applesauce until that wayward can of garbanzo beans is restored to its proper place. This "gotta fix it now" urge, usually aimed at others, can work *for* us when we use it to jump-start apologies.

Try it with your young (or not so young) 'uns. If you don't receive at least one hug in return, you can choose between having your kitchen cleaned or your ironing done, and I will selflessly volunteer Dr. Chuck Lynch to do it. (Now, where *did* I put his phone number?)

CHAPTER TWELVE

Post-Project Depression (Stretch Marks Not Included)

Ever heard of the baby blues?

Symptoms include disturbances in eating and sleeping, trouble concentrating, and crying easily. That goes double for the mother. When her symptoms intensify or last more than three weeks anytime during the first year after delivery, chances are she has crossed from the blues into postpartum depression.[1]

Maintaining my characteristically pure scientific methods of research (spamming friends with E-mail), I found that 100 percent of Marthas surveyed reported varying degrees of post-*project* depression. Symptoms mirror those of postpartum depression, but without the lingering smell of sour milk.

MARTHA BUDDIES SING THE BLUES

— Shawnee, after moving to a different apartment, spent an entire day cleaning the oven. "When I finished the project eight hours later, my back was screaming for relief and my arms and legs had already given up the ghost. The sparkling oven is still sparkling because I rarely use it. Who would want to go through that again!"

— Lynn jumped at the opportunity to design a complicated brochure for her favorite networking group, even though she was already overloaded. By the time she was finished, she wasn't even sure she wanted to be a member anymore. "Stress just sucks the joy right out of a plum project. I should have let this particular opportunity pass."

— Teri coordinated a major conference in only three months. What happened when it ended? "I just crashed all day in a blob. My life seemed strangely empty. I missed the excitement of the adrenaline rush. I felt restless without having the conference to think about. I felt exhausted from the effort and somewhat filled with regrets of what I wished I would have done better."

— Lori had an inability to say no to church volunteer work. "It wasn't just one overnighter, but a series of lots of things. I felt so good about my volunteering and did *way* too much." (The details of her near-fatal burnout are in chapter 15.)

— Deanna directs a weekend leadership retreat annually for 250 high school students. "Afterward, I have to re-enter reality as the rest of my job and life just keep on going with the same expectations. I spent a month gearing up for the retreat. I spent the week prior in high gear with all the details. I spent the weekend troubleshooting and enjoying being the one 'in charge' (Martha in her prime, I suppose!). I get all the 'thank-yous for all you do to make this happen,' then go home to an empty house, wondering, 'What now?' My body runs on adrenaline and the rush of putting it all together, then when it's all over, I just feel kind of lost and lonely. Like I need to find another mountain to climb to feel like I'm doing anything worthwhile. It's just a weird, empty feeling."

— Sheryl, who got remarried between chapter 11 and this

one, attempted an extensive remodeling job with her new husband on his vintage house. Results: "We eventually threw out the paintbrushes and said forget it. Don't *ever* do a remodeling job in a new marriage, especially with a blended family in tow. I was totally depressed. The more we tried to fix, the more we found to fix. We ran out of money shortly after we ran out of sanity, and still haven't regrouped."

THE CYCLES OF LIFE

There's the rinse cycle. (Don't forget the fabric softener.) The menstrual cycle. (Don't discuss it in the presence of small children. They'll just beg to take turns riding it.) And the post-project depression cycle. (Don't think any Martha is exempt.)

As you read the phases of the post-project depression (PPD) cycle, recall the opening chapter where I described how my former co-worker, Teresa, and I cleaned the storage room.

Phase #1

Martha notices an area needing improvement. A grandiose gleam comes into her eye. She imagines the finished project becoming the benchmark by which all others will be measured (and come up short). The key characteristics for this stage are *overoptimism* concerning how wonderful the project can be and *underestimation* of what the project will take. Still, Martha is eager to dive in.

Phase #2

Martha acts immediately, extremely, and independently. She may not waste time getting official permission. Once a project is begun, Martha wants to hit it hard until it's done and done right. She will deny herself breaks, meals, and even sleep in order to reach her goal of bringing perfection to the needy area. To Martha, her body's not a temple—it's a rocket.

Phase #3

Martha thinks irrationally. As she works, she imagines how the completed project will reduce stress and save time in the long run because it will be *done forever*. The project itself snowballs, pushing Martha into progressively smaller details and higher standards. She imagines how people will gratefully admire her skill and sacrifice, even if only between trips to the break room for doughnuts.

Phase #4

Martha savors the finished project. Beyond "job well done" satisfaction, this is a literal rush for a productivity junkie. Martha loves the kudos, too. "You did great. It looks really good. We needed someone to do this for a long time." But people tend to have short memories of others' accomplishments. They will not tiptoe around the manicured perimeter of Martha's project forever.

Phase #5

Martha collides with reality. Her project becomes outdated, begins to deteriorate or ("How *dare* they!") is criticized! Sleep deprivation has skewed her perspective. The intense expenditure of physical and emotional energies has depleted her chronically low reserves. Martha's feelings are very close to the surface. She can't help but conclude that, for all that she invested, she got very little in return. None of this is what she expected.

Phase #6

Martha becomes depressed. She feels anger toward those who do not revere her project and moans, "Why do I even bother? I'm the only one who cares." Martha may feel betrayed by the project for being imperfect after all she devoted to it. Finally, she may also feel disappointment in herself for being unable to sustain a hyper-productivity mode such as she enjoyed at the project's peak.

MISSION: RECOVERY

The term PPD may be new, but the phenomenon is not. Thousands of years ago, someone went from a mountaintop project to the valley of burnout. God's prescription for the prophet Elijah then is good for us Marthas today—a recovery period during which he ate, rested, and relaxed.[2]

I don't know why this never occurred to me before. Once it did, my PPD lessened significantly. Here's how it works: After every demanding project, I schedule—and take—a recovery period. The more demanding the project, the longer the recovery period. The time isn't to catch up all the other things that were neglected during my all-consuming project. The recovery period is for me. My body needs recharging, my spirit needs restoration, and my relationships with God and people need renewal.

Too often our criterion for food, rest, and leisure is what's fast; what will interfere the least with our projects. That may be efficient, but it's never healthy and seldom satisfying.

Nutritious and Delicious

Suppose I wave under your nose a heaping plate of tasty "country kitchen" food worthy of a Norman Rockwell painting. Now, choose between eating that or an entire bag of candy. Both may fill you, but only one will satisfy you.

Eat for satisfaction! Junk food snarfed during a project frenzy may fill our stomachs, but it won't satisfy us. Nor will it give our bodies the right fuel to function at top form. Healthy food will do both.*

Choose to Snooze

Marthas tend to have so many sleep problems that I've devoted all of chapter 15 to them. Essentially, we need to increase the

---

* I'm not the only Martha to serve cereal to my family for dinner when I'm maxed out with PPD. One evening, I noted how bland the oat cereal and toast looked. My mother's words came to mind: "A healthy meal has a variety of colors." I made a mental note to buy Froot Loops.

hours of sleep at night and overcome reluctance to power nap during the day.

Sleep for satisfaction! Sleep deprivation for the sake of working on projects will fill our sense of productivity, but we'll face the next high-demand day drained.

At Ease, Please

Too many of us use breaks merely as cues to switch tasks. Time for a coffee break? We make phone calls and photocopies. Time for lunch? We run errands. Time for the weekend? We do housework and laundry.

Relax for satisfaction! A break should be enjoyable, energizing, or both. (Chapter 14 goes into this more.) It's also important to reconnect with people during this time, so include them in your leisure plans, too.

Define the Lines

Eating, sleeping, and relaxing for satisfaction help cure PPD. Defining the lines of how far we should go for the sake of a project helps prevent a relapse.

Marthas often have difficulty discerning which tasks merit self-sacrifice. For example, we may give all of the following equal magnitude.

— Throwing oneself on a land mine to save comrades
— Diving into frigid waters to rescue a drowning child
— Slaving nonstop for two weeks to prepare a home video montage for Uncle Fred's retirement party

Frequently we reach PPD because we've neglected healthful boundaries. A boundary isn't a barricade to keep us from reaching success, but a hedge to keep us from leaving health. Our grand plans for a project may spur us to plow through the hedge by skipping meals, rest, and relaxation. It's much better to lower our lofty goals and work within the green borders of healthful boundaries.

What are alternatives to crashing and burning over Uncle Fred's video? Taking up a collection among the family to have it done professionally. Sharing the work among several relatives. Or, if we want to get really radical, doing something less intensive but just as meaningful.

Healthful boundaries are an essential preventative against PPD. Plus, then we won't be so devastated upon discovering Uncle Fred accidentally taped a *Gunsmoke* marathon over the whole thing.

A SECRET DOOR

Years ago, I thought the answer to being maxed out and overcoming PPD was more strength. Then I discovered the answer lay in a paradox. Our faith is full of them, you know. If we want to be first, we must be last. If we want to be wise, we must become fools. If we want to be strong (and what Martha doesn't!), we must become weak.[3]

This does not make sense to Marthas. We'd rather forge ahead harder and faster; bulldoze down obstacles through the force of our will; commandeer our bodies to do more than they were designed for. No, we Marthas have little tolerance for weakness in anyone—especially ourselves.

But weakness is not an obstacle. It's a blessed boundary to keep us mindful of who is God and who is not.

Doing great things for God is not the heart of the spiritual life. It is not leaping tall buildings in a single bound, not flying faster than a speeding bullet that attracts God's blessings. It is, rather, coming to the end of our own resources—it is recognizing our need and asking for help—that is the beginning and foundation of the Christian life. The biblical text is clear about the spiritual meaning of our weakness. God's strength is made perfect in our weakness. This is no mere Hallmark one-liner. It is one of the foundations for all spiritual growth. . . . It is when we lean into our weakness rather than running from it, that we experience things unimaginable in the safety of our comfort zones. . . . Contrary to all of our instincts, then, the neediness which can be so terrifying to us is, in reality, the opportunity which makes it possible . . . to begin the healing process.[4]

135

How can the remedy for our weakness be more weakness? Joni Eareckson Tada became a quadriplegic after a diving accident in her teens. Here's her view:

> My disability is my greatest asset in prayer because it forces me to bed early where, once I'm lying down, I have several hours to meditate, think, and reflect. . . . It is the most wonderful "Mary" time for me, a "Martha." I don't know that if I were on my feet I'd have the discipline to carve out this amount of committed time in prayer— this is why I "boast in my affliction": it provides for me time which, otherwise, I might not devote to the Lord.[5]

We can get angry at our limitations, or we can "lean into them" as Joni did. When we do, we'll find that our weakness is not a brick wall between us and our plans. Our weakness is an open door to God, who says, "My grace is enough; it's all you need. My strength comes into its own in your weakness."[6]

A MARTHA MENTOR

Roxie Ann Wessels, a godly grandmother, shares with women's groups her story of PPD which happened in her forties.

> I had brought it on myself foolishly with poor judgment. My days were filled with "gotta get this done—that done—this list—too much to do—not enough time." I had run past the yellow light of caution. The result? Sleepless nights, panic attacks, and depression.
>
> With God's Word as my lifeline and His Holy Spirit to teach me and lead me, I began to face the truth about my over-doing and over-extending. "Ye shall know the truth and the truth shall make you free." I invited God to remove the camouflage, the self-deception, and the pride that said, "I'm strong. I can do all these jobs. I'm in control."
>
> Perfectionism had its roots in my childhood. I sought to be acceptable to God in my strength and effort—just as I had with my parents.

OK, we know where she *was*—right where many of us are today. But she didn't stay there. Roxie Ann continues:

Let me tell you about my healing.

Every night for two years, I refused to dwell on negative thoughts and began to fill my mind with thoughts of God and His Words.

I then bent my will—my knees—consciously toward praise, the dwelling place of God. Soon I began seeing the best in situations rather than the worst! And I began to thank Him for the gift of laughter! The gift of humor!

Then, I had to accept the unfulfilled. There is so much we will not get done! In a sense, this whole act of surrender—of acceptance —determines our level of Christian living.

In time, God made me the whole person He wanted me to be.[7]

Richard Swenson, author of *The Overload Syndrome,* shares his view of PPD.

When stress is pushed to extremes, burnout results. Next time you go into a forest, take a small sapling and bend it over. When you let go, the tree will straighten back up again. Now take the same sapling and bend it until it breaks. When you let go, it cannot straighten back up. This is a picture of burnout. In the same way, in our lives, we adapt and adapt and adapt—and then something inside us snaps. When this happens, healing comes slowly. I personally do not believe we ever get back the same level of enthusiasm, innocence, and passion that we previously had. Yes, there is life after burnout. But most of the healing is by scar formation.[8]

TRUTH OR CONSEQUENCES

Currently hosting *The Price Is Right,* Bob Barker also used to host a TV game show by the name of *Truth or Consequences.* When it comes to projects, Marthas also have a choice that goes by the same name. We've looked several times so far at how deception is integral to the maxed-out lifestyle. In fact, there are more lies linked to our Marthaness than to a congressional hearing.

Not sure what I mean by that?

Jesus said, "You will know the truth, and the truth will set you free."[9]

Hmm . . . I never felt free after finishing a project. I felt drained, disappointed, and defensive. Maybe that's because I was operating from a lie instead of the truth. Remember, freedom comes from truth.

Many Marthas perceive their worth as being only as good as their last project. This is a lie. Our worth is based on Christ alone. He's everything we'll never be, and yet He freely shares His identity with us. *That's* the source of our worth. I heard an elderly preacher say, "If you want to know how much I'm worth, ask the One who bought me."* When we live this truth, we'll be free from the enslavement to perform perfectly. Neil Anderson says, "Too often we try to change our behavior without changing our beliefs. Nothing will change your behavior more than a true knowledge of God and who you are as His child."[10]

If we can get a grip on this, life will cease to be an empty series of projects that leave us progressively more exhausted. Life will become an abundant path of freedom, joy, and health that energizes us to know Christ as He intended.

A SATISFIED CUSTOMER

Writing this book has been a huge project; at times an all-consuming project. And yet now, as I approach the deadline, I don't feel tense, irritable, or on the verge of a major crash-and-burn PPD. I'm excited! Upbeat! Medicated!**

Sure, I'll take a recovery period after mailing the final draft, but it will be much shorter than previous ones. Why? Because I paid better attention to boundaries now than I did in the past.

Well, OK. There *were* a few late-nighters, but no all-nighters, and I always slept late the next day. A few Froot Loop dinners, but not many, and I always served a hot meal the next time (assuming Pop Tarts qualify). Honestly, sometimes a major project *does* require changes in our eating, sleeping, and relaxing. It's just so much easier

---

 * I would've shouted, "Amen!" but it wasn't that kind of church. A nod and a smile were allowed, but only on Sunday nights when the service was informal.
 ** Seriously, there are times when Marthas have pushed themselves so long for so hard that rest alone won't help. If PPD continues for more than a few weeks, talk to a doctor, trusted clergy, or professional counselor.

to get back on track when those changes in our boundaries are *temporary* and *minimal*.

Compromise is OK. Surrender is not.

And now, if you'll excuse me, I'm going to put a juicy roast in the oven for dinner, my feet up on the couch, and read the latest Mitford book.

Care to join me?

CHAPTER THIRTEEN

Holidays, Schmolidays (Or, Six Hours One Wednesday)

One Thanksgiving Eve, I smiled in welcome at unexpected guests while plotting how to get rid of them.

After spending three hours that Wednesday shopping and cleaning for the traditional feast at my house, I finally wrestled my little pilgrims into bed. Next on the list: an all-night kitchen stint to bake four pumpkin pies and modify a dinner roll recipe to surpass last year's "Plymouth Rocks." With luck, I could catnap before dawn. But when the doorbell rang, my plans for a happy holiday fluttered away like dry autumn leaves.

"Hi!" Barb bellowed as she, her husband Leroy, and their rowdy twins elbowed through my front door. "Just thought we'd *drop in!*" That term prompted a glance outside to see if they had taxied up in the Enola Gay.

Within seconds, my almost-asleep children bounded from bed

to offer bags of candy corn reserved for tomorrow. Within minutes, toys covered my living room and my tongue bled from biting
it. And after an hour of hinting, "This is not a good time for a visit" and "I'm sorry I can't offer you coffee," I popped the question.

"Barb, don't you have to get ready for Thanksgiving dinner tomorrow?"

"Not this year and what a *relief!*" she crowed. "We're going to
my in-laws' house so I don't have to cook or clean or a *thing!*" She
smiled and patted her husband's hand. "Tonight, we're just going to
relax and *enjoy* the holiday."

"Not at my house, you're not! Can't you take a hint? Now
pick up these toys, pack up your kids, and hit the road!" I said in
my dreams for weeks to come. At the time, I collapsed with silent
disbelief into a chair. Barb mistook my catatonic gaze for unblink-
ing interest and kept babbling. Her family departed eventually,
leaving wall-to-wall clutter in their wake.

Anger overcame exhaustion for the fifth hour. I sugar-detoxed
the kids and put them in bed (again), scooped up toys (again),
straightened pillows and chairs (again), vacuumed (again), wiped
off sticky fingerprints (again), and finally made it to the kitchen to
start cooking.

There, I discovered that I had forgotten to buy evaporated
milk. I called my working husband and asked him to get four cans
after his shift. He bought condensed milk instead. Experienced
cooks know this will not work. I accused him of having a condensed brain and stormed out to buy evaporated milk myself. I
desperately roamed dark streets looking for the last open store
with the last can of evaporated milk in the metro area.

A FLY IN THE EGGNOG

What is it with holidays anyway? As a kid, I loved them! As an
adult, I dread them. Somewhere along the way, a change happened
and I think I know just when it hit.

About five years ago in June, my daughter spotted the first
Christmas decorations of the season at the mall. Well, OK. It was
mid-October, but I still thought it was way too early.

"Mom! Look! Christmas!" she cried between gasps. She ran ahead to gaze at the festive display while I trudged behind, pushing her then-infant brother Andrew in his stroller.

"Oh, Mom, just think!" Elizabeth continued breathlessly, reaching out to finger the decorations. "Soon we can bake cookies, and buy presents, and send beautiful cards, and decorate the tree, and put lights up, and I'll be out of school, and company will come over, and you'll fix a big Christmas dinner, and . . ." At least that's what I think she said, because right after "bake cookies" she lost me. Her idea of baking cookies is to set up a command post in the kitchen for three days and bake until the oven melts down. Of course, I have no one to blame for that except myself because that's the way I used to approach the holidays—no detail too small because after all, *it's Christmas* and all the hard work is for *my family* to show how much I *love them.*

Being older and wiser (and, yes, tireder), I tried a different tack.

"Hey, Elizabeth! Let's try something new this year. Let's get some of the refrigerated dough that we can slice and bake."

Elizabeth wheeled around to face me, her eyes and mouth wide with shock.

"*Mom!* Then it wouldn't be *Christmas!*"

Help. I've created a Martha.

BEYOND MAXED OUT

Somewhere, we Marthas got the idea that on holidays our usual overextended, overcommitted, maxed-out selves should be stretched just a little bit further.

Not only are our homes supposed to be clean and orderly at all times, but they must also be decorated in a tasteful and coordinated holiday theme from room to room.

Not only are our meals supposed to be healthful, hot, and on time, but they must also be augmented with traditional favorites and seasonal delicacies—all from scratch, too.

Not only are we supposed to keep up with regular paperwork, but we are also supposed to send a personal greeting, professional portrait, and clever newsletter to everyone we've ever known re-counting all the blessings of God in the past year.

Not only are we supposed to maintain a budget as good stew-ards, but we are also expected to give generously to charities and purchase meaningful gifts for everyone from the baby-sitter to the organist from our cousin's wedding nine years ago.

Not only are we supposed to be perpetually young, thin, and beautiful, but we also need a sparkling holiday dress for the corpo-rate office party and matching family outfits for quiet evenings at home sipping cider in front of the fire.

Not only are we supposed to be involved in regular ministry, but we must also lead a children's choir, cook for the homeless shelter, and herd sheep for the church's musical extravaganza. And if we fail in just one teensy, weensy area, then the entire holiday is ruined for everyone.

This leaves me with just one question: "Sez who?"

Who came up with all this "stuff"? All these *ought to's, need to's* and *shoulds?* C'mon! Give me someone to blame so I can vent my anger! How about blaming the media? That's very popular these days.

Women are shown juggling a myriad of responsibilities with the pa-tience of Job and the wardrobe of a fashionable "best dressed" nomi-nee. From her moussed hair to her manicured fingernails, the typical TV heroine has it all together. Her leather pumps never break stride, not even when fitting holidays into an already full schedule that may combine homemaking with an outside job.

Women, who typically are responsible for the details of holiday celebrations, are put under additional pressure by magazines whose covers boast the ultimate in entertaining. The inference is that with just a few dollars invested in purchasing this magazine, any woman holds the key to making the best Christmas [Thanksgiving, Easter, Fourth of July] that her family has ever known. What the printed matter fails to say is that the twelve-course dinner, five-tier cake, and seventy-three handmade gifts were done weeks in advance by a paid staff of professionals! Not surprisingly, then, women who expect such feats on their own become frazzled, angry, depressed—burned out.

Television and radio talk shows also share tips on creating warm holiday memories. Suggestions abound for quick-easy-inexpensive dishes, decorations, and gifts. Are such suggestions realistic? Is there a hidden message in these programs that women who do not personally design meaningful family traditions are failures? Sometimes the implication is that children will always have an inner void because their moms never dressed liked Pilgrims on Thanksgiving or hand wove their Easter baskets.[1]

Are you shouting, "Amen!" I am! Finally somebody understands the pressure put on women at the holidays. But right or wrong, even blaming the media doesn't fix the problem. And the problem is, Marthas don't just get maxed out during the holidays —they get *mega-maxed*.

What's the solution? Let's review some of the things we've learned so far about our shared perfectionism and then apply them to the holidays.

1. Perfection is an illusion.
2. Truth sets us free; lies keep us in bondage.
3. God's love for us is based on His character, not our performance.
4. Our innate abilities are gifts to be used within healthful boundaries.
5. Only one thing is needful.

Applied to the holidays, these five points work out practically like this:

1. *Perfect holidays are an illusion "perpetrated" through the advertising and entertainment industries.* Fun to watch, useless to strive for. One of my favorite holiday videos is the classic musical, *White Christmas.* The last time I watched it, I noticed how many unrealistic details it has. Once Bing Crosby and Danny Kaye's characters team up after the war, not one thing goes seriously or permanently wrong. The movie ends with every loose end neatly tied and warm fuzzy feelings as plentiful (and fake) as the last-minute snowflakes.

2. *Put every* ought to, need to, should *message to this test: Is it*

true? For example, is it true that you must decorate your entire home in a coordinated theme for the holidays? No. That is not true. Decorations are optional. Repeat all this aloud ten times daily if needed. It is possible to observe holidays in meaningful ways without a single ornament, candle, centerpiece, or lighted lawn display. (If your family protests that "It's just not Christmas!" then begin a re-education program on what it really is. Somebody has to break the cycle of unrealistic expectations for the sake of future generations. It might as well be you!) Remember that truth sets us free and lies weigh us down. When you begin to feel weighed down by holiday tasks, examine the "why" behind them. More than likely, the whys are lies.

3. *Our imperfections are built-in.* Permanent. (In this life, anyway.) You know, it's kind of interesting that an infinite, holy God has lower expectations than we do. For His own Son's birth, God thought a small, dusty stable would be just fine. If God had asked a Martha to get His Son's birthplace ready, there would've been months of frantic preparation, decorating, delegating, and overspending. In the end, Martha would still wish she'd had more time, more room, more help, and more money. That's because megamaxed Martha missed the point: God doesn't want to evaluate us, but to enjoy us! Would you enjoy a relationship with a frenzied, preoccupied person, or with one who thought just being in your presence was the best thing in life? Yeah, me too.

4. *Our natural perfectionistic abilities often attract offers for projects.* As Marthas, we love the attention, too. "No one takes care of details like you do. Would you please take over the Easter pageant this year?" Remember what we learned in chapter 12 about how the lack of boundaries leads to burnout. Prayerfully plan your holidays in advance with your family. When offers start coming in, you'll be prepared to say, "I can help with costumes for the next two weeks, but after that I'm booked" or even the daring "I won't be able to help at all this year but thanks for asking." Say yes when it's right to do so, but always draw a boundary around it.

5. *What is the one needful thing of whatever particular holiday you're facing?* If it's "To make everyone happy," then please go back to points number one and two! For Christians, the one needful thing

of the major holidays is to acknowledge God. Do your holiday preparations acknowledge God or credit card companies? God or keepsake ornament manufacturers? God or the rivalry between you and your sister-in-law over which one sets the prettiest table? The enemy of perfectionism wants to splinter your focus into dozens of unreachable and temporal peripheries. Keep your focus. Keep your focus. Keep your focus. Just one thing is needful. Remembering this will stretch the holiday meaning beyond mere Kodak moments into eternity.

MILKING IT

I guess my expectations were just too high. For some reason, I supposed that in a major metropolitan city of a half-million people, somewhere a grocery store would be open *and* stock plenty of evaporated milk. No such luck.

Heading home, I griped about every stupid holiday on the calendar and having to do everything myself. Then I caught a glimpse of my angry expression in the rearview mirror. How could I, a normally loving wife and mother, harbor such a stinky attitude and then preach thankfulness to my kids? I parked the car in the driveway and sat. "God," I prayed, "I don't feel thankful. I'm sorry, but that's the truth. Please show me just one thing to be thankful for tonight."

A moment or two passed and the sixth hour ended. Here's what I noticed. My well-running and paid-for car. A not-fancy but still warm-and-waiting home. Happy and healthy kids safe inside. A forgiving husband. A starlit night. Crisp November air. A new calm in my heart.

This year will find me better prepared. But if you come to my door on Thanksgiving Eve, don't expect me to let you in. I'll be too busy counting my blessings . . . and my eighty-seven cans of evaporated milk.

CHAPTER FOURTEEN

Hurry Up and Relax!

Coo, those English chaps are weird.

Like clockwork, they put the skids on a perfectly good day of stress and deadlines to sip tea through their stiff upper lips. They contaminate it with cream and serve it with little cookies called "biscuits." Don't they know cream is meant only for coffee? That biscuits are supposed to be split open and drenched with pork gravy? Has no one told them that slurping strong java while continuing to work is more efficient?

The English tea ritual is something I always viewed much like an ultrafrilly pink dress: prissy and repulsive. Taking breaks of any kind seemed irresponsible, selfish, and wimpy. Like a firefighter who, while battling a raging inferno inside an orphanage, looks at his watch and says, "Oops! Time for my break!" and then saunters off in search of a sandwich.

This "take no breaks" thinking peaked during my stint working in communications. I skipped both breakfast and midmorning breaks. I worked through lunch most days, and instead snarfed a granola bar at my desk. Many were the afternoons when I punched my time card out at 5:00 P.M., but then worked off the clock until late evening. At least one Saturday a month (if not two or three) found me in the office again.

My husband listened to me complain about the workload, but told me to relax and think of it as job security.

Working nonstop wasn't confined to the business environment. Oh, no. I pulled many all-night cleaning stints at home, particularly when either a holiday or company was due the next day. Sleepy-eyed, Neal would shuffle to the basement at 3:30 A.M. (where I was ironing and folding the cobwebs before I put them in the trash) and ask some *ridiculous* question like "Are you coming to bed yet?" or "Do you really need to do that right now?"

If you're a maxed-out Martha who hasn't been asked this question yet, it's only a matter of time until you will be. To prepare for how to answer it, memorize the three possible replies below.

— "But I'm almost done."
— "This needed to be done anyway."
— "If I don't do it, it won't get done."

SPECKS AND BEAMS

Most people, when they're working too hard, realize they need a break. Often, they go completely crazy and actually *leave* at day's end—even though the work isn't finished.

"Boy," they'll say, wiping their brow. "I'm all tuckered out. Think I'll call it a day, get a hot meal, some sound sleep, and come back at it tomorrow, rested and rarin' to go. See ya!"

Not Marthas.

Why stop working when we're so close to being done? Never mind that *done* is like the horizon: We always see it, but never reach it.

Besides, by skipping breaks we Marthas can defend our titles as Tireless Workers, Dedicated Servants, and Pains in the Neck.

What? Who said that? Who thinks we're a pain in the neck? Don't others notice our sacrifice? Aren't they inspired by our example? Don't they secretly wish they were as capable as we?

If you want to know what others *really* see when they look at a maxed-out Martha, read this and try not to weep.

— *Snippy manner* ("Hurry up! We should've left 3.7 minutes ago!")
— *Clenched jaw* ("Why am I surrounded by incompetence?")
— *Furrowed brow* ("Don't bother me when I'm thinking of all the things I have to do!")
— *Bloodshot eyes* ("I found a mistake when I proofread your proofreading of this three-hundred-page report last night.")
— *Hunched shoulders* ("Only I can do the cooking, cleaning, shopping, laundering, ironing, carpooling, diaper changing, checkbook balancing, dog training, gardening, decorating, Christmas newsletter writing, and roof repairing correctly.")
— *Facial tic* ("Twitch? What twitch?")

Not exactly Miss America material. Everything about us *screams* that we need to take a break.

But do we notice?

No.

Does everyone else?

Yes.

There are plenty of possibilities why we won't take breaks. Competitiveness. The need to be needed. All-purpose false guilt. Warped humility that says we don't deserve a break. Certainly there is some carryover from the Puritan work ethic that lauds productivity and shuns relaxation. Leisure was equated with idleness, and we all know whose workshop that is. And there's still that pansy ambiance of the proverbial tea break.

My favorite reason is simple: We are project-oriented rather than people-oriented. We don't want to interrupted by anyone—*including ourselves!* We often ignore our bodies' needs and have tunnel vision on the task before us. This is why many Marthas skimp on meals and sleep, refuse breaks, and consider a forty-hour work-week as a part-time job. Remember, too, that workaholics aren't confined to the corporate world. There are plenty of die-hard Marthas burning themselves out as mothers, homemakers, home-schoolers, elder-caregivers, ministry workers, classroom helpers, and church volunteers.

STICKS AND STONES

"Quick—without looking it up—how many of the Ten Commandments can you name?"

This is the question I asked the Martha Buddies. Teri was the first to respond. Here's what she said:

No other gods before God.
No idols.
Honor father and mother.
Don't steal.
Don't take God's name in vain.
Don't commit adultery.
Don't be a false witness.
Don't murder.
Don't covet.
Oops, I'm missing one. Knowing me that is probably the one that is most important! . . .Oh, the Sabbath! That's telling that I forgot that one!

Yes, Teri, it *is* revealing that the commandment to observe the Sabbath is the one you overlooked. It's also the one several other Martha Buddies omitted.

More revealing is the attention God gave to the fourth commandment about resting one day each week—135 words worth. Commandment number six ("You shall not murder") is only four words. God used *33.5 times* as many words to tell His people to rest than to tell them not to kill each other.[1]

Moses recorded the story of someone who just couldn't take a day off. The price? Death by stoning. *(Yikes!)* All this person did was gather wood on the Sabbath, and yet the result was execution. Why? Because in God's eyes, the sin wasn't picking up a few sticks, but *lust*. God said, "[Don't] prostitute yourselves by going after the lusts of your hearts and eyes."[2]

Our Christian subculture typically associates lust with sex, money, and power. But according to God, lust can occur with anything. Lust is a craving that demands satisfaction. It cares neither for cost nor consequences. Sort of like a spoiled teenager with Daddy's credit cards.

When we Marthas push ourselves past healthful boundaries on a project because we "crave" perfecting it, finishing it, doing it quickly, or mastering it, we have become lustful. We've lusted for perfection, completion, efficiency, and control. Is that what the stick-picker lusted after, too? Maybe these thoughts rolled through his mind during a Sabbath stroll.

Look! In front of me! The finest firewood I have ever seen. Dry, not too dusty, and the perfect size for my needs. Too bad today's the Sabbath and work is forbidden.

Maybe if I pick up the best pieces and hide them behind this rock, it wouldn't be considered work. There. Now I won't have to fight the usual post-Sabbath crowd either.

But wait! What if someone finds this pile before I can return for it? Maybe I should take it home after all. The distance isn't far enough to violate any law.

I know! I'll set aside one-tenth of the wood to give to the priests. If there is a penalty, which I doubt, it will probably be something small, like a couple of doves. I can afford that.

Praise God, we are no longer under Old Testament rules! When Jesus came, everything changed. As the Lamb of God, He became the perfect sacrifice for every sin. When we blow it now, we don't need to follow a ritual to buy temporary forgiveness. Nor do we need to fear stoning. Yet Marthas who are assured of unlimited grace through Christ can become numb to the seriousness of rationalizing sin. According to God, that includes refusing to rest.

And there's still a price to pay.

RELAX OR DIE

Among the Martha Buddies who shared their stories of what refusal to relax has cost them, Shawnee's is the most dramatic.

★   ★   ★

After years of unknowingly clenching my teeth when I was tense, my facial muscles had become so tight I could hardly open my mouth wide enough to fit in a toothbrush, let alone a spoon. Mealtime had been reduced to Jell-O and mashed potatoes. My continued inability to relax eventually created a change in my jaws. No longer just a dental situation, [it became] a medical situation called avascular necrosis, which meant the tightness of my muscles had cut off life-giving blood circulation for the bones, and they and my facial structure were deteriorating at a terrifying rate. . . . Three surgeries later, my lower face was so changed several old friends didn't recognize me, but I was relatively pain free, and my jaws had been saved. These days, when I look in the mirror and see my $60,000 rebuilt reflection, I can't help but wonder if turning my problems over to God instead of worrying would have saved me those years of pain.

★   ★   ★

Don't clench your jaw? Me neither. But an inability to relax is still hurting our bodies. To get the specifics, I spent six hours doing research in a medical library. My conclusion: The most harmful thing one does to one's body is spending six hours in a medical library. Do you have any idea how boring it is in there? Not only was it appallingly deficient of fiction, it had no videos, compact discs, books on tape, or story hour. Still, the restroom was clean. I even saw one of my doctors in the periodical section reading *Today's Spleen,* although I suspect it was camouflaging the latest issue of *Affluent Golfer.*

I found that a life of all stress and no rest is a bad thing. A very bad thing. Over and over, references popped up to Hans Selye, the father of stress research and a Canadian endocrinologist who devised the "General Adaption Syndrome" to show how the human body responds to stress.[3]

There are three stages in Selye's description. The first is *alarm reaction.* When faced with stress, the human body wants to "fight or flight." This sets off an internal chain reaction that amounts to nothing short of a "physiologic alarm." The second is *stage of resistance.* The human body can maintain this level of adaptation for months or even years, but extended resistance leads to *stage of exhaustion.* The prolonged strain on various organ systems exacts its toll and, voilà, stress-related illness occurs[4] to the tune of billions of dollars annually, most of which is spent on subscriptions to *Affluent Golfer.*

A medical writer summarized Selye's theory as "anything that causes stress endangers life unless it is countered by an adequate adaptive response."[5] Did you catch that middle phrase? *"Unless it is countered . . ."*

Here's a radical thought: Maybe, just maybe, the Creator of the universe actually knew what was best for our bodies when He commanded regular rest. Not resting will do more than make us crabby. It will make us sick. It might even kill us.[6] Faced with prospects like that, we would be wise to accept regular breaks both during our workdays and longer ones on weekends.

Just don't do it in a medical library.

TEA FOR ME

My opinion of English tea breaks changed after my husband took me to the local Highland Games, an annual festival celebrating Scottish heritage. There, a small persistent inner nudge began. Maybe it was prompted by the bagpipe music, which had never made me teary before. Maybe it was the Braveheart wanna-bes wandering about in kilts and chucking small telephone poles around that actually made me consider buying plaid yard goods. Maybe it was finding our name's origin on the Irish map, which made me ashamed at having called Michael Flatly "Lord of the Dunce." (I know it wasn't the aroma of haggis.*) But somehow the

* Haggis (pronounced HAG-us) is a traditional Scottish dish, thus expanding the Scot stereotype of being thrifty to include being the *least* picky eaters on the planet.
"Angus, m'lad! Have ye no sense? Toss that beef brisket to the dogs and

latent genes from my British ancestors awoke and guided me toward a booth stocked with teapots.

The Brown Bettys are squat, round, and stamped with "Made in England" on the bottom. The busy, windblown woman running the booth was not. She was, however, authentically and thoroughly British and showed classic unruffled patience with my American criticisms of and questions about tea. The Brown Bettys, traditionally a glossy, deep red-brown, are touted as the best vessels for making "proper English tea." Skeptical but obedient to the inner nudge, I left the booth with a hunter green teapot, a floral tea cozy, a box of Yorkshire Gold tea, and instructions from a foreigner.

I followed the directions precisely the next morning. I heated water. Twice. I steeped tea. Once. I poured. I added milk and sugar. I sipped. And then . . . I was converted. Or perhaps *reverted* is a better word. At last, the genes of my English great-great-grandfather Thomas satisfied their silent longing for proper tea. Warm, sweet, creamy tea. Sipped at leisure every morning from a dainty cup. Drunk at leisure from a steaming mug every afternoon. Tea that simultaneously calms and energizes. Tea, glorious tea.

A friend gave me a colorful gift book on tea. Just looking at its lovely cover soothes me. The author shares recipes for scones, techniques for folding napkins, and themes for tea parties. That woman is really into tea!

Someday, I might try those ideas. But for now, *this* woman is into relaxing on the run. I don't have time to iron authentic Irish linens for each place setting. Instead, one arm sweeps the Legos, puzzles, and newspapers to the end of our big dining room table— and the tea is on.

As I arrange cups, spoons, milk, and sugar on the half-cleared table, the thoughts of my family are happy ones. Instead of wishing they'd *get away from me* so I can get more work done, I'm eager to *get*

---

bring me the cow's liver, heart, and lungs. And donnae wrinkle your wee nose at me, ye ungrateful bairn!"

"I'm sorry, Ma. But I nay cannae eat those unless ye boil them in the cow's stomach with plenty of lard."

"Oh, aye . . . but just this once!"

For better or worse, this is how haggis has been made ever since. Braveheartburn, anyone?

them over to me so I can love them. I know they'll be so surprised and pleased when I finally call, "English tea!" that they'll do a very un-Martha thing: They'll stop midproject and come running to relax.

Taking tea isn't the point. Grabbing an oasis is. We can teach our kids to be little workaholics, or we can teach them to listen to their bodies and take regular, spirit-soothing, body-restoring breaks.

RELAXING ON THE RUN

The key is to *make breaks as different from work as possible.* Vary the location, the body position, the activity level, the senses used—everything! Whether we're constantly on our feet or trapped behind a desk, there's something from the Martha's Dozen below to help us relax.

1. Speed-walk.
2. Toss a Frisbee.
3. Power nap.
4. Listen to soothing music.
5. Listen to an audio book.
6. Listen to nothing.
7. Window-shop.
8. Get a massage.
9. People-watch on a bench.
10. Do a series of slow stretches.
11. Eat at someplace out of the ordinary.
12. Buy yourself a flower.
13. Sit in a library.
14. Sit in a church.
15. Take a long lunch and see a matinee.
16. Invite someone special to meet you for coffee or tea.
17. Spend time in one small area of a museum or gallery (don't feel compelled see it all in one visit).
18. Go to the zoo or pet store—without the kids!
19. Take a meandering drive in the country with the windows down.

20. Arrange with a friend or co-worker to meet for a picnic, swapping the sack lunches you've both packed.
21. Do a relaxing handcraft.
22. Drink plenty of water.
23. Eat a healthful snack.
24. Spritz the air in your work area with a pleasing fragrance when you return to it.

Still not convinced to relax? Come 'round, luv, and have a spot of tea with me. You'll find it's ever so delish, especially with these dear little biscuits.

CHAPTER FIFTEEN

Work Now, Sleep Never

Alicia, a college friend of mine, provided childcare in her home in addition to caring for her two preschoolers and infant. Translation: messy house. Alicia wasn't a slob; she just lived smack-dab in the middle of a nonstop, demolition diaper derby.

Late one evening, after the day-care kids exited and her own little ones yielded to sleep, her husband, Devon, asked when she was planning to go to bed.

"I can't go to bed at all tonight," she answered.

"Why not?" (Devon walked right into this one.)

"Have you forgotten? Your family and mine are coming over tomorrow for a cookout. I have to finish the laundry, clean the entire house, run to the all-night supermarket, fix potato salad and baked beans, make a cheesecake, do a relish tray—"

"Sweetheart! Don't do all that tonight. You're already exhausted."

"But if I don't do it, it won't get done."

Devon draped his arm over Alicia's tired shoulders. "Tomorrow's a big day, and you need your rest. Come to bed now," Devon promised, "and I'll help with everything in the morning." His pleading and patting continued for several minutes before Alicia reluctantly gave in.

She awoke early the next morning to find Devon gone. At first, Alicia thought he had driven their only car to the supermarket for her menu's ingredients. But hour after hour went by, and still no Devon.* Alicia tried to make a dent in her to-do list, but with all the kids underfoot not much got—or stayed—done.

Devon finally returned home about fifteen minutes before all their company was due.

"Where were you?" she shrieked in panic as soon as he walked in.

Devon had the nerve to ask, "What are you so upset about?"

"What do you *mean* what am I so upset about?" Alicia's voice rose to one notch below dog-whistle frequency. "You *promised* to help me get everything ready for our company! You talked me into *sleeping* last night instead of working, and now I'm not ready! The house isn't ready! The food isn't ready! *Nothing is ready!*"

"The car's ready."

Alicia's bulging eyes did a slow, unbelieving blink. "The car?"

"Yeah, come outside and look at her. I've got her all washed and waxed. Even shampooed the upholstery. The tires and oil were OK, but she needed a little wiper fluid—"**

No wonder we Marthas have a hard time sleeping. On the few occasions when, against our better judgment, we are persuaded to rest, we usually regret it.

---

* Are you wondering why Alicia didn't try to reach Devon on his pager or cellular phone? It's because he didn't have them. No one did. Back then, we thought clock radios were high-tech. "It's got AM *and* FM? Far out!"

** If this story sounds familiar, maybe it's because you saw Devon and Alicia on one of those televised divorce court programs. Devon was the guy with a steering wheel around his neck.

"SOMEBODY NEEDS TO WASH THESE SHEEP"

It's inevitable. When we're maxed out, sleep becomes a problem. Traditional "tricks" to induce slumber fail. And, if you've ever seen (and smelled) a woolly flock in person, you'll never try to coax sleep by counting sheep again.

Many times sleeplessness is self-inflicted, as Alicia had planned. Need more hours in the day? Steal some from the night. These regular withdrawals from our health bank eventually catch up with us, though. Deanna shares, "When I'm low on z's, I get physically sick very easily. I eat healthily, exercise regularly, but if I go a night or two without much sleep, I pick up whatever's going around! And if I don't sleep well, I'm cranky with my students."

The tip-off for Lynn that she's sleep deprived is that she begins to think, "My husband's irresponsible, my kids are brats, and the cat won't stay out of my way." And yet, she describes herself as a reverse junkie. "I hate to go to bed, and I hate to get up. What a dichotomy. I'm refusing to give my body what it needs. Besides, I'm a night-owl Martha who's overstimulated during the day. Nighttime is the only time when no one is making demands on me."

Seems Sheryl and Teri are the only Martha Buddies who haven't had trouble with sleeping. The rest of us, though, have struggled not just with going to bed at night, but with sleeping when we finally do lie down. Shawnee says, "My main problem with sleeping is that my brain refuses to quit thinking." Hmm. This sounds almost exactly like what Lynn told me: "Even though my body wears out, my brain keeps thinking of more things to do." All the *ought to, need to,* and *should* messages play on a continuous loop in our maxed-out minds, fanning the flames of urgency, tension, and anxiety. No wonder we can't sleep!

Because Marthas typically push themselves so hard, almost every Martha suffers from some degree of sleep deprivation. Dr. John Shepard Jr. of the Mayo Clinic's Sleep Disorders Center suggests a radical idea: Instead of using an alarm clock to wake us in the morning, we need a sleep bell to tell us to go to bed at night.

"Turn off the TV; turn off the Internet," says Dr. Shepard. "For perfectionists, what they should be doing is obtaining the amount of sleep per night on a regular basis—same bedtime, same wake time—that allows them to feel fully awake in the daytime. Waking up should be spontaneous because you got enough sleep. You are overriding your intrinsic biological requirement for sleep if your alarm clock is waking you up."[1]

The Epworth Hospital in Melbourne, Australia designed a scale to measure sleepiness. Ironically, it's called the Epworth Sleepiness Scale.[2] Because I found it on the Internet and no one in a lab coat was nearby saying, "This won't hurt a bit," I jumped right in and got tested.

Eight scenarios popped up on my computer monitor and required me to rate how likely I would be to doze in each one. Sounds simple, but I flunked. Whoever wrote this test didn't give me enough details! For example, I was asked if watching television would make me nod off, but that depends on what I'm watching. If it's a thrill-a-minute, romantic comedy adventure mystery, then no, I'm not going to fall asleep. If it's the nightly farm report ("Pork bellies are up two-tenths of a point, while milo futures hold steady"), then color me unconscious.

The best indicator of how we sleep at night is how we live each day. Cranky? Tired? Blue? Welcome to womanhood. Add, for two weeks or more, memory loss, poor concentration, and trouble operating heavy machinery,* and say hello to insomnia.

"IT'S A SIGN!"

Those symptoms all point to insomnia. Insomnia, in turn, points to something else because it's not a disease or condition—it's a symptom, too! But what's the root problem manifesting itself through sleep problems? These are probably the first things that come to the minds of most Marthas.

Self-diagnosis #1: "I can't sleep because my circadian rhythms are off." What are circadian rhythms? These are the more than one

---

* To me, *heavy machinery* is a relative term. Sure, there are days when I'd have as much trouble maneuvering a backhoe as the next woman. On other days, even my blow-dryer qualifies.

hundred patterns in our bodies affecting cycles of sleep, hormone production, blood pressure, and more every twenty-four hours. (These are not to be confused with *Canadian rhythms,* which are the random impulses to don a flannel shirt, eat forty pancakes, and then chop down the nearest tree.) We tamper with our circadian rhythms when we deprive ourselves of ample sleep, natural sunshine, regular meals, and even social breaks.[3] If we're guilty of all that, then we can add insomnia to our list of other health complaints. But we still haven't found the root.

Self-diagnosis #2: "I can't sleep because I have a chemical imbalance." Deep in the hidden recesses of the human brain lies the pineal gland.* This gland makes melatonin, a hormone that sets our body clocks. Production is usually triggered in a natural way by nightfall,[4] but, thanks to Thomas Edison, we don't have to go to bed at night! We can stay up for hours and hours and hours, thus confusing our poor pineal glands and further gumming up the sleep works. Even if we pop melatonin pills every night (which the medical community strongly cautions against), we've just temporarily alleviated a symptom, insomnia. And, again, we still haven't found the root.

Self-diagnosis #3: "I can't sleep at night because I have too much to do." This was the situation Lori found herself in. "I remember when my kids were very small," she said, "and I didn't sleep night after night. I would walk around [during the day] in this mental fog. I started getting sick all of the time and wound up in the hospital with spinal meningitis. It wasn't that the kids were waking me up; I just had insomnia. I was trying to do too much while I was raising my precious little ones." Every Martha knows the burden of "The List That Won't Die." In our heart of hearts, we believe the "one thing" truly needed is a completed list! Yet no matter how hard we work to cross things off, more appear. It's like housework and paperwork. Just when we think we're done—poof! There's more! Why can't that happen with the good stuff instead, like

---

* Pronounced *PY-nee-al.* Coincidentally, this is also where our deepest secret lies buried—our true weight. Clerk at driver's license bureau: "Tell me your weight." Me: "Never! You'll have to get past my pineal gland first!"

birthday presents and chocolates? Even so, endless lists aren't the root of insomnia.

MORE ROOTS THAN ALEX HALEY

Who needs to count sheep? There are so many possible roots of insomnia that we can count them instead to induce drowsiness. Insomnia could be triggered by something as simple as the bedroom's temperature or as complex as unresolved emotional issues. ("Therapy, anyone?") Because I don't want to try counting indictments either, I'll leave formal diagnoses to medical professionals.

What I can do is share what I believe is the key factor in sleeplessness among Marthas: deception. Author and counselor Neil Anderson points out that, as Christians, we *know* when we're being tempted (Yell at an inconsiderate driver . . . or let it go. Watch a sleazy TV program . . . or change the channel. Sacrifice sleep for work . . . or go to bed.), but we *don't know* when we're being deceived. That's why the seeds of lies and half-truths take root so easily.

Temptations usually involve choice: A or B. Deception obscures choice. This is something we've seen before. Deception led Eve to think there was a shortcut to perfection. Deception led Martha to an obsession with externals instead of a focus on the eternal. Deception leads us to buy into imperatives that are non-negotiable. We *ought to* be the ultimate woman, wife, mother, and Christian. We *need to* keep immaculate homes. We *should* maintain an impressive career or ministry. We *must* nurture everyone around us into happy, healthy, holy people. We *have to* do it all, be it all, all the time.

When enslaving statements like these pop into our minds or come out of our mouths, let's ask one question: "Why?" Then let's keep asking why until we get to underlying deception. Remember—most of the time, the whys are lies. Once they're identified, we can counteract them with truth and be set free.

Unchecked, "The List That Won't Die" syndrome can turn into *listeria*. (Several Marthas in the same room can lead to *mass listeria*.) This is the state of near-panic associated with never-ending tasks and their attached expectations—very few of which truly belong there. Listeria is a major detriment to sleep. Lori realized this later. She says, "I wish someone would have told me, and that I would have given myself permission to just take care of my small ones, who were only seventeen months apart. I was doing a lot of good things in my church,* but in hindsight I can now see that the world and the church would have gone on [without me]. *I allowed my fear of what other people thought about me to dictate what I did and didn't do"* (Lori's italics).

"Perfect love casts out fear."[5]

Truth sets us free.[6]

When we live the *truth* that God's *perfect love* for us is based on His character and not our performance, the fear will fade. In its place will come calmness, security, and rest—and those make great bedfellows.

"ROCKABYE, MARTHA"

Now that we've got fresh help for our minds and spirits to settle down for the night, it's time to help our bodies snooze.

You've probably heard the usual advice about insomnia: Avoid caffeine, big meals, and rich foods in the evening. Rise at the same early time every morning, even if you don't feel rested. Be physically active through each day. Don't get hooked on sleeping pills. Get up and do something boring instead of tossing and turning. See your doctor if insomnia lasts more than two weeks.

---

* You've got to read Lori's list to believe it.
"I was directing a youth choir/puppet ministry, which involved thirty teenagers every week and taking them on tour all the time. I led a weekly women's Bible study. I supervised the child care area at the YMCA. I worked there so I could take the kids with me while I worked. I was president and treasurer of our Sunday school class, which meant I took care of the monthly fellowship time and kept track of the moola. I was a youth sponsor and went to senior high youth group every week, along with all of the other activities they did. I was in the choir on Sundays and sang on the worship team Wednesday nights (which involved two weekly practices). I worked one day a week at Mother's Day Out and taught a class of four-year-olds. Plus everything else that goes along with being a pastor's wife and mother of two little ones. That was definitely a period of insanity for me!" Folks, this is in addition to doing all the holidays and also having moved several times! Praise God, Lori's free at last from feeling compelled to perform.

Have you "been there, done that" with those textbook tips? Consider three fresh ideas I've gleaned from my on-again, off-again struggle with the sandman.

1. *Determine the downhill hour.* This is the time each day when my energy supply and the demands upon it are most out of whack. Not sure when it is at your house? A strong indicator is when your child calls, "Mom!" and instead of cooing, "Yes, my precious little love bunny?" you snap, "NOW WHAT!" It's all downhill from there.

What does this have to do with insomnia? If I insist on the usual Martha-high standards of conduct and cleanliness during the energy ebb, stress becomes infectious. Soon everyone in my family is snapping at each other, avoiding one another, and then having trouble falling asleep. Only recently did I discover the connection. When I did, the solution was obvious: Lower my standards.

Anything I can do to facilitate relaxation for my household during the downhill hours is worth it. If it means eating leftovers on paper plates, good. If it means turning a blind eye to the laundry and clutter, fine. If it means not harping at every infraction, great. My kids love it when, after dinner, they're not drafted for chores or abandoned while I "do it myself," but instead are invited to spend time with their dad and me. Sometimes we play dominoes, complete a puzzle, or read books until bedtime. We all have an easier time falling asleep when the evening hours end on grace notes rather than sour ones.

2. *Get ready for bed before dinner.* Late one night, I shuffled toward my bedroom in that delicious drowsiness that promised instant sleep. But first, I had to wash my face, brush my teeth, and change from my clothes into my pajamas. After I did that, I was wide awake! Then it hit me. My go-to-bed routine was almost identical to my get-out-of-bed routine. Every morning, I wash my face, brush my teeth, and change from my pajamas into my clothes. No wonder my mind and body were confused!

Since then, my "wake up" and my "get sleepy" routines are as different as possible. Early bed-readiness also gives me a slight boost in alertness, which in turn helps me get through the downhill evening hours. When bedtime finally rolls around, there's no delay between me and the hay. Besides being more relaxed for the evening, I'm automatically excused from last-minute shopping. ("Sorry, Son. I can't get rhubarb, a Slinky, and jumper cables for your science project because *I'm in my pajamas.*") Being jammie-clad also reminds me not to start any big tasks that might tempt me to work into the wee hours.

Marthas can't go from sixty to zero in five seconds. We need extra time in the evenings to downshift . . . then slow down . . . and then stop. An early pj period is just the ticket.

3. *Create a boudoir.* The whole strategy of moving toward being happy and sleepy at bedtime fails if my bedroom looks like a test site for nuclear missiles. Shocked? Don't be. While other parts of my home may have been picture perfect, my bedroom wasn't. For years I had a pattern of overcleaning my house, beginning with the basement and working my way up. By the time I reached my upper-level bedroom, not only had I run out of cotton swabs for polishing the woodwork, I was zonked.

The problem was further compounded by my nightstand. All the unpleasant chores I hated—clipping coupons, dating photos, answering mail, and mending clothes—accumulated there into precarious piles. "I'll work on these a little each night," I told myself. At least that's what I think I said. I wasn't really listening at the time. Anyway, it was hard to fall asleep with a towering guilt-generator just inches from my face.

Not only did I remove those projects from my bedroom, I erased all signs of anything related to work, parenting, or stress. The room still isn't fancy, but it's clean, uncluttered, and cozy. The hidden benefit of going to sleep in a comforting environment is waking up in it, too.

Do I do *all* three of these things *all* the time?

Nope.

But when my old Martha behaviors do a number on my slumber, I don't panic. For me, these tips *work*—usually within just a few nights.

"BUT I'M STILL NOT SLEEPY"

Don't want to count sheep? Don't want to count the possible causes of insomnia? Try counting the number of times you've heard this: "Salvation is the gift of God." The Marthas I know can preach that with the best of them, emphasizing how a gift must be accepted before the recipient can benefit from it.

Salvation isn't the only gift God has given to us. Sleep is His gift, too. Dr. Richard A. Swenson writes in his popular book called *Margin,* "The need for sleep is undeniable and should be regarded as an ally, not an enemy. To sleep soundly for a full night is a valuable restorative gift."[7]

If you still have trouble with going to bed at night or slumbering well once you get there, here are some choice words: *Jesus slept.* Go and do likewise, counting your blessings all the way.

CHAPTER SIXTEEN

Buckle Up! We Are Now Entering Reality

I have a confession to make: I fantasize about the neighbors I wish I had.

Now, don't get me wrong—I like the people currently living around me. But you know Marthas. We can always think of a way to improve things.

On one side of my dream home, I want Aunt Bea. You remember her—the live-in relative of Mayberry's sheriff, Andy Taylor. Never mind that she's a fictional character of an old television show. Disregard that the actress who portrayed her, Frances Bavier, has gone to that celestial syndication in the sky. This is a fantasy!

Anyway, little Opie has grown up to become a famous movie director with no time for country bumpkin relatives. Andy married that nice schoolteacher, Helen, and they're spending their retirement traveling in a motor home. Poor Aunt Bea just pines away, wishing she had someone to fuss over. (This is where I come in.)

One day, Aunt Bea pops over to share some of her apple crumb pie. I show her a chapter from a novel I'm writing and she sees at once that my talents are wasted on domestic chores.

"Now I won't take no for an answer!" she declares, her chins raised defiantly. "I absolutely insist that you let me come over tomorrow and straighten up a bit. It won't take me any time at all and it would make me so happy."

Soon after, Aunt Bea takes my family permanently under her ample wings. She arrives each morning with glorious flowers from her garden and three scrumptious home-cooked meals. After she cleans my entire house, she goes home (taking our laundry with her, of course). I feel a tad guilty about it, but who am I to deprive a senior citizen of the one thing that brings her joy?

On the other side of my house in fantasyland live Shari Lewis and Lamb Chop. I loved watching them on *The Ed Sullivan Show* in the 1960s, and my kids loved watching *Lamb Chop's Play-Along* thirty years later. Shari lives again in my fantasy and pleads with me to allow my kids to spend all their free time at her house.

"Please!" she says. "I've worked with kids all my life, but never have I met any as precious and adorable as yours. I beg you to grant me joint custody!" Of course I give in. How can I deny such a perceptive woman?

Across the street lives Oprah Winfrey. Even though she's two cents away from being a billionaire and has a talk show audience so adoring they were mesmerized by her on-air pedicure, she still has time for me. We get together every week at her house for brunch.

"You've got to give me more ideas for my show!" she implores. "And please write the foreword to my next book. It would really help with sales." I'm reluctant, but finally agree when she insists on putting my picture on the cover.

My fantasy goes along just fine until I think of Mr. Rogers. It's pretty hard to think "neighborhood" and not think of him too, but he's the one person I won't let in. Don't you think it's a little strange that this guy *visits his own house?* Every day, he comes in his own front door and greets countless strangers who are already there. (Can you say, "Trespassing"?) Even weirder, when the day is done, *he's* the one who leaves! Hardly a good example for impressionable kids.

At this point in my daydream, the whole fantasy-thing goes sour. Then my eyes refocus on reality. My house is trashed most of the time. We eat lots of bargain take-out. My kids are frequently bored. The last time I had brunch was . . . was . . . Tell me again what "brunch" is?

"EASY DOES IT"

This phrase, from popular twelve-step recovery programs, serves to remind members not to rush progress; to pace themselves as they test new ways of thinking and doing. But if a Martha ever devised a recovery program, it wouldn't dillydally through twelve long steps. Hers would get to the point—and fast:

Step 1:   Admit your problem.
Step 2:   Snap out of it.

Easier expected of others than applied to ourselves.

Being maxed out is a hard way to live. Because we didn't get here overnight, we can't expect that even a delightful read of an exceptionally insightful and humorous book (feel free to nominate me for a Pulitzer) to be an instant fix.

Hiring an entourage of assistants might be a quick answer, too, but few of us have the budget for that. Training them would be a waste of time anyway because (a) it would be faster to keep doing everything ourselves, (b) there are labor laws against working people that hard, and (c) they'd just complain about the uniforms.

Maybe running away is the solution. Wouldn't it be wonderful to break away from all the demands, projects, and responsibilities? To be utterly carefree and relaxed? To lie on a quiet beach (having applied plenty of sunscreen), swim in a crystal-clear lagoon (having waited at least one hour after lunch), or browse a rustic market (having pinned our traveler's checks securely to our underwear)?

Hmm. Escaping from a life of maxedness* may be harder than we thought!

LEAVING ON A JET PLANE

My health has crashed a few times from being maxed out—once requiring admittance to a hospital. Because overwork had weakened my body's immune system, I was unable to fight off a virus. Talk about being weak! From my hospital bedside, my husband offered me water, and the effort it took for me to lean forward, sip through the straw, and lean back again left me exhausted.

I do not want that to happen again—to me *or* to you.

Below are a few things I've learned the hard way. I beg you to take heed! Yes, change is hard; even heartbreaking. Any woman who's had to find a new hairdresser knows that. But change can also be a turning point, and that's what this book offers to you.

1. Set a Departure Date

Instead of being the hardest, this first step is the easiest! It's simply choosing a point on the calendar by which our present obligations will either expire or lessen. From that date on, nothing new gets added to replace what's finished. But it won't work unless we *tell* everyone and then *follow through.* The idea of doing this occurred after my hospital dismissal. Several months later, I worked up the nerve to set a date and then announced it to the world.

At a loss for words? Try this: "Beginning June 1 [or whatever date you've chosen], I will wrap up my current obligations and be unavailable for any new ones until further notice."

Not one person I told expressed disappointment! Most told me they not only thought this was a smart move, but secretly wished they could do likewise. Just in case, be prepared to get selfish responses such as, "But that doesn't include the [Christmas

---

* One of the few perks of being a writer is inventing words like *maxedness.* Here's another new one: chocolating, as in, "Sweetheart, I'm *chocolating.* Please go get a half-gallon of triple-fudge ice cream." Be sure to say it in that special tone of voice between "threaten" and "whine" for fastest service.

pageant/annual performance reviews/homeschooling fair/family reunion] that you've coordinated every year . . . does it?" There's only one way to answer questions like that: "Yes."

2. Pack a Parachute

Depending on how maxed out we are, we might have to bail on some projects before they're done. I know that's a shocking thought, but how badly do we want to break free? How serious are we about protecting (or salvaging) our relationships? How much longer can we avoid crashing our health? Just the thought of possibly having to eat hospital food should be motivation enough. If further incentive is required, move bailing from the mental category of "Things I Have Never Done Before" to the "Things I've Tried at Least Once" category.

Sometimes bailing isn't an option. In that case, let's simplify. For example, if your livelihood depends on finishing a work project, schedule (and take!) a vacation when it's over. Be really radical and ask for an assistant, a transfer, or a demotion when you return. Maybe a career change is needed. Let focus—not money—be the prime motivator.

Are you a stay-at-home mom who can't bail either? Cheryl Gochnauer, author of *So You Want to Be a Stay-at-Home Mom,* advises, "Be careful to avoid the super-stay-at-home syndrome that says you should sew like June Cleaver, bake like Betty Crocker, volunteer like Mother Teresa, and clean like the scrubbling bubbles. Instead, focus."[1] (There's that word again!) Remember—you're a stay-at-home mom, not a stay-at-home maid.

We are not indispensable. There are just as many situations that we *can* bail from as those we can't. For the latter, start squawking (nicely). If no one has offered help to us before, maybe it's because we gave the impression of being invincible. (Or maybe we were so bossy and demanding no one wanted to get near us.) Barbara Hemphill, paper tamer and organizational expert, says it best: "Asking for help is not a sign of weakness, but of wisdom."[2] Besides, one of the ways God shows His love for us is through good friends in times of need.

173

In the meantime, both corporate and domestic Marthas can jettison excess obligations in other areas of their lives. We all need to enlist the support of people who love us to cheer us on and help us keep our scaled-down focus.

3. Take Off

Welcome aboard Martha Airways, the airline that's always on time and seats every passenger alphabetically!

Seriously, our journey from maxed out to freedom is an important one. This downtime of healing and recuperation is what our spirits, minds, bodies, emotions, and relationships have been yearning for. But even more than being a recovery period, this is a *discovery* period.

Writer Jean Fleming says, "Throughout the ages, Christians have struggled to discern the proper balance between the cloistered existence and the life of reckless, zealous ministry—between bustling service and sacred hush. . . . We become caught in the Mary-Martha dilemma, weighing the active life with the contemplative life."[3]

Marthas need no help in discovering the active life. It's the contemplative one that troubles us. (Pause here if you need to think about that.) Yet when we slow down, our spirits can connect with God as He intended. Then we discover that sitting at His feet isn't a boring obligation, but a blessed essential.

If you can't take your discovery period all at once, do it in installments. Set aside a regular time at *least* once a week, if not daily, to debrief and detoxify yourself inside and out. Drink lots of water. Listen to praise music. Watch a sunset. Meditate on Scripture. Review your perspective to see if it focuses on eternal or temporal things. Fast or eat only natural foods. Look at the stars. Develop accountability with someone. Worship. Doing these things puts you a heartbeat away from living your life according to the "one thing" principle.

When will your discovery period end? I don't know—I'm still in mine! I submerge and emerge based on the demands of life and how well I'm handling them. Like me, you may always be susceptible to Marthaness, but—praise God!—none of us has to be subject to it ever again.

RAVE REVIEW

"I just need to lower my stress level. Then I'll fee bine. I mean, be fine."

That's true to a degree. Stress is undeniably a major problem, but it isn't the root of all our Martha woes.

I've said it before, but it bears repeating: A good part of the blame belongs on deception. False beliefs about our identity, our worth, and our purpose keep us in bondage—weighed down and overwhelmed—to perfectionism and overcommitment. True beliefs about our identity, our worth, and our purpose keep us free—energized and victorious. Want less stress? Have more truth.

Believe me, you and I are both going to be tested on this. Therefore, I'm offering below a review of the lies we need to avoid and the truths we need to embrace. We saw these first in chapter 8, and we've been learning them throughout the book; here they are in an at-a-glance format. Study well!

Lie #1   If we tried harder, we could get everything in our lives under control. Then life would be perfect and we would be happy.

Truth #1   Perfection is an illusion.

Lie #2   All those inner imperatives (the ought to, need to, should messages in our minds) are true. If we achieved them, our pressure and stress would go away.

Truth #2   Truth sets us free; lies keep us in bondage.

Lie #3   God's love for us fluctuates based on our performance.

Truth #3   God's love for us is based on His character, not our performance.

Lie #4   We should use every ability we have to the utmost at all times, even if it harms us or someone else. After all, didn't Christ suffer for us?

Truth #4 Our abilities are gifts from God to be used within healthful boundaries.

Lie #5 Everything is equally important and urgent.
Truth #5 Only one thing is needful.

How exactly will we be tested? It might not be anything obvious, like "accidentally" bumping into our high school trigonometry teacher who "just happens" to have a midterm examination with our name on it tucked inside his pocket protector. Most tests are choices.

— When our schedule is already full, will we accept or turn down another responsibility?
— If we accept it, will we work within healthful boundaries and then let it go, or will we overextend ourselves and neglect relationships for the project's sake?
— If we turn it down, will we feel guilty and inadequate, or will we pat ourselves on the back for keeping our focus?

STUDY GUIDE

Having struggled in the Martha mode for years, I finally found two tips that help me pass these tests on whether to max myself out or not: (1) *no fast answers* and (2) *creative compromises.*
Here's a sample test disguised as a compliment.

"The [project manager/ministry coordinator/whatever] is unable to finish her job because she [retired/had triplets/was kidnapped by Bigfoot]. We are desperate for someone to help us out and you were the first person who came to mind. Your skills would be just perfect, and we would feel so relieved to know the entire thing is in your capable hands."

Now watch the one-two punch of *no fast answers* and *creative compromises* in action.

"Thank you. I'll need at least a week to think about it. In the meantime, please check out alternatives such as [using a temporary agency/promoting the assistant to this position/reading a *real* newspaper]."

During the waiting period, pray about it *and* review your personal mission statement (described in chapter 17). Does this new offer support your focus or sidetrack it?

After the week is up, ask how the investigation into alternatives went. It's likely that these "desperate" people haven't done a thing because they assumed that, as usual, you'd rescue them. Maybe they did check out other options, but still consider you to be their number one choice. What will you answer? Yes? No? Another creative compromise? I was about to write, "You're on your own with this one," but then I realized that's not true. The same God who gave you identity, worth, and purpose in Christ will help you to keep your focus.

MIRROR, MIRROR

Back in chapter 8, we looked at the original perfectionist—Lucifer. When he decided God's perfection could be counterfeited, he overlooked something else: It can also be reflected.

Here's how it works. A mirror has no image of its own. We have no perfection of our own. Instead of fabricating a fake, outward perfection—an endless, impossible, and exhausting task—you and I can reflect God's authentic perfection. The real thing! How do we do this? By thinking and acting in accordance with His character.

1. *God is perfect truth.*[4] We reflect that not by operating from lies, but by thinking on, acting in, and speaking truth.
2. *God is perfect love.*[5] We reflect that not by withholding affection when we're displeased, but by loving ourselves and others unconditionally.
3. *God is perfect mercy.*[6] We reflect that not by being judgmental and bitter, but by extending extravagant compassion.

4. *God is perfect grace.*[7] We reflect that not by rationing pity, but by showering reckless benevolence.

5. *God is perfect peace.*[8] We reflect that not by clenching control, but by surrendering to His sovereignty.

Are you thinking, *But if I let go of control, everything will fall apart! If I forgive someone who's not repentant, she'll never change!* The point is this: We're not God. (Surprise!)

This is where our sister Mary can help us. If, like her, we sit at the feet of Jesus, we'll have done more than chosen the good part. We'll have moved close enough to reflect Him.

★   ★   ★

Remember the fantasy I started to share at the beginning of this chapter? In my dream neighborhood, my home bordered those of Aunt Bea, Shari Lewis and Lamb Chop, and Oprah Winfrey. Then Mr. Rogers came along, bringing reality with him—a reality that's far from perfect.

But, hey, this is life. This is real. My days are full of chaos and clutter and kids. And the most important part, I now realize, is contained in the first four words of that sentence: *My days are full.*

So what if life is imperfect? Live it and love it anyway! And on days when it's hard to do either, you can borrow my fantasy. I'll deliver it myself and we'll talk about it over brunch.

CHAPTER SEVENTEEN

One
(More)
Thing

What right did Martha of Bethany have to be maxed out?

Granted, compared to ours, her world was small and its demands much less. There is no scriptural mention of Martha having in-laws, emotional baggage, power lunches, software glitches, car payments, cholesterol worries, appliance repairs, difficult children, hot flashes, or junk mail.

We Marthas of the New Millennium have all that and more. (Although I will allow that preparing a meal for the Son of God might be a *tad* stressful.)

What was it that Martha needed? What is it that we need? Is it balance? Is that the "one thing"?

THE HARDEST SHOW ON EARTH

The king of balance may be German acrobat Karl Wallenda. He and his family astounded audiences with high-wire feats. Their most memorable: the Great Pyramid, three tiers made of seven people. Patriarch Karl said, "Being on the tightrope is living; everything else is waiting."[1]

Marthas would say, "Attaining balance is living."

Our dream is to achieve perfect balance. That elusive formula by which every cog in every wheel fits precisely and moves smoothly. Balance implies meticulous organization of all factors. An unwavering reserve of time and strength. The unflagging cooperation of people. And no room for surprises.

If we could just achieve perfect balance, we could add another tier of goals and projects. When that tier is balanced, we, being the accomplishment addicts that we are, could add another . . . and another . . . and another.

But balance is a tricky thing. Once attained, it gives the appearance of ease. Ever notice how those high-wire performers look so composed? They may stand or sit on the wire nearly motionless, but that doesn't mean they're resting. No, the hard part is far from over. Once perfect balance is attained, *it must be maintained*. Every fiber of each performers' being is utterly consumed with preserving perfect balance. Is that what we really want? Intense, life-or-death exertion with no room for error? Not me. Especially if I have to wear those tights.

RIGHT IDEA, WRONG APPROACH

OK. So our lives aren't balanced and probably never will be. Here's the next question we each must ask ourselves: "Is my life simple or complicated?" DUH! Our maxed-out lives are so complicated they make the tax code look like a cookie recipe.

The apostle Paul feared that some believers had lost their "simplicity and purity of devotion to Christ."[2] Since when has devotion to Christ ever been simple, especially for Marthas?

We may try to scale down and simplify. But we inevitably sabotage ourselves with our habit of *self-imposed complexity.* Here's what I mean by that.

An unidentified Martha was asked to handle her fifth-grader's Thanksgiving party at school. The simple thing would have been to buy treats and play musical chairs. But would this satisfy a Martha? No. Instead, I made a big production out of it. I mean, *the unidentified Martha* made a big production out of it. She baked authentic pilgrim corn cakes from a description in a library book. On her computer, she designed bingo cards for twenty-five students, using holiday terms instead of numbers. " 'Mayflower.' Anyone have 'Mayflower' on their card? Good. Isn't this fun? The next word is 'starvation.' "

One simple task just can't stay simple with us. Our *self-imposed complexity* stretches things to the extreme at any cost. Having no sense of when we've reached "good enough," we not only over work, we overparty! It's one of the fastest ways to being "distracted with much serving."

While simplifying may not be the "one thing," it's definitely a good thing! It is key to leaving the maxed-out lifestyle, and I highly recommend it. But what is the *criterion* for simplifying? There has to be a *reason,* a *guideline* for deciding what stays and what goes; for where the line between "good enough" and "maxed out" lies. And that brings us even closer to the "one thing."

PMS: OUR NEW BEST FRIEND

I know what you're thinking: "Premenstrual syndrome. Bring on the potato chips and leave me alone."

Actually, PMS in this case isn't that monthly reminder of why we all hate Eve. It's a *personal mission statement.*

Marthas are never without a list, mental or actual. It's full of things that we must do (or think we *need to, ought to, should* do). The PMS, though, isn't about *what* we do. It's about *why* we do. In a word, it's focus.

Imagine that you called a local radio station to identify the mystery song in their latest contest: "Muskrat Love" by The Captain and Tenille.* The disk jockey says, "Congratulations! You've won a trip! Get packed because your plane leaves in an hour!"

After a few minutes of jumping up and down, you pull out the suitcases, and then . . . what? Because you don't know the destination, length, and purpose of the trip, you are clueless about what or how much to pack. Just to be safe, you throw in a little of everything—ski boots, sundress, blue jeans, power suit.

This is how many of us Marthas spend our lives. One woman commented, "We're often worst enemies to each other. When we see someone packing inordinate activities into her week, we sigh in admiration instead of asking, 'Why are you doing all this?' "[3]

The result is an overloaded, maxed-out life full of distraction—no traction. The smell of burning rubber and the sound of a racing engine fill the air. Very impressive. But we haven't budged an inch. Our wheels are spinning for lack of that single focus on which, in order to advance, we must grip.

How to Discover Our PMS

When you were a kid, did you have one of those tiny plastic, water-filled snow globes? You could shake it up and watch plastic snowflakes swirl wildly, then drift to the bottom, revealing a plastic scene of some kind.**

Discovering our PMS amid the commotion of our maxed-out lives is impossible. Like the snow globes, we need to be still long enough for our working and thinking and doing to settle. At first, the snowflakes will continue to swirl madly. Keep sitting and listening. Then they will twist and swoop for a bit. Keep sitting and listening. Finally, the snowflakes will drift downward and lie undisturbed. It's at this point of calmness and quiet that our sitting and

---

* Driving with my kids one day, I burst into a song from the 1970s, "Knock Three Times," by Tony Orlando and Dawn. Don't ask me why because I didn't like that song even when it was new. As I bebopped down memory lane and knocked on the dashboard, Elizabeth reacted. Giving me her best horrified-teenager expression, she said, "Help. I think I've been oldied."
** Usually Santa Claus driving his reindeer: Dasher, Dancer, Prancer, Blitzen, Sleepy, Dopey, Goofy and Alfred E. Newman.

listening truly begins! It may take an entire day, or a week, or even a year to reach this point. But when we do, the scene—*our focus* — will be revealed.

During this settling period, we must pray. Have others pray for and with us. We must meditate on Scripture. Most of all, we must worship, lifting our hearts, minds, and voices in prolonged praise to God.

There are great resources out there to aid us in discovering our focus. One of the best is *The Purpose-Driven Church* by Rick Warren.[4] He uses the SHAPE acronym, which is wonderfully applicable to an individual looking to discover her purpose. It stands for *spiritual gift* (see related Scriptures[5]), *heart* (what is your passion?), *aptitude* (what are your skills?), *personality* (what is your style?), and *experience* (what have you done and learned?). Willow Creek Resources has published an excellent course, too, called *Network: The Right People in the Right Places for the Right Reasons.*[6]

Some Marthas may be tempted to bypass the sitting and listening part and just dive into these books in order to speed things along. Here's a travelers' advisory for such ambitious Marthas: Doing so alters the snow scene into a dangerous blizzard and obscures visibility. *Stillness is a prerequisite to finding focus.* Neglect it at your own peril.

Top Five Lists of the PMS

We know our personal mission statement needs help if:

5. It's carved in stone.
4. It's so complicated and all-encompassing that we're back to being maxed out.
3. It neglects our relationships with people.
2. It neglects our relationship with God.
1. We're so proud of ours that we judge those who don't have one.

We know our personal mission statement is fine if:

5. It's on paper, so we can review and revise from time to time.

4. It expresses *one* purpose (or focus) in *one* sentence.

3. It nurtures our relationships with people.

2. It nurtures our relationship with God.

1. We realize that having a PMS is not a sign of superiority over people, but of submission to God.

Our PMS provides focus. Focus is what we walk on, lean against, and look through. Focus keeps us on track, at peace, and in tune. If opportunities presented to us compete with our PMS, let's say no. Every no we say to a nonessential focus-stealer is a big yes to our PMS. One of the best ways to keep our sanity, our peace, and our health is to keep our focus.

Balance is impossible. Simplicity is important. Focus is imperative.

We're getting closer, but we still haven't reached the "one thing."

WHAT HAVE WE GOT TO CHOOSE?

My childhood home had a huge yard filled with trees—a willow, some cottonwoods and evergreens, a cherry tree, a plum tree, and a couple apple trees. Those were my favorite to climb. Their bark wasn't as scratchy as the cottonwoods, and their sturdy limbs allowed me to disappear high among the verdant leaves. So what if the apples were small, green, wormy, and sour? Not much good for eating, but great for lobbing at targets.

Years later, my mother-in-law took me to Illinois for my first official apple-picking experience. When I spotted from a distance the trees in the orchard, I almost fell off the hay wagon. They were puny! A fraction of the size of my hometown apple trees! If a child dared to clamber up one of those, the spindly branches would snap like toothpicks. Poor Mom Stack had been hoodwinked by the world's scrawniest apple orchard.

Then, as we walked among the trees, my opinion changed. Every tree dangled luscious, softball-sized, ruby fruit in abundance.

We each bit into an apple, leaning forward to let the warm juice drip off our chins onto the grass. Glorious!

Why the big difference? The trees in my old yard didn't have a focus. They'd been going their own way long before we moved in. The trees in the orchard *did* have a focus: to bear fruit. The orchard owner pruned away ruthlessly so all the nutrients went toward that single focus.

Being maxed out may look impressive—we're important! Talented! Needed! But, like my apple trees back home, the skimpy fruit of Marthaness is basically useless.

Writer Jean Fleming used the analogy of a tree to describe her focus finding. Her relationship with Christ was the tree. The limbs were the major areas of her life. The branches on those limbs were the tasks she was doing in those areas. How did she choose which branches to prune? She chose between those "which bear fruit and which merely use nourishment."[7]

What in our lives is merely draining nourishment?

What in our lives is bearing fruit—or *could* bear fruit if more nourishment were diverted in its direction?

Choosing between the two may be difficult, but it's what we must do.

Jesus wanted Martha to *choose* as Mary did; to *choose* as He Himself did after a night of prayer when He selected twelve men to be His closest disciples. The original language for this kind of choosing is "not necessarily implying the rejection of what is not chosen, but 'choosing' with the subsidiary ideas of kindness or favor or love."[8]

When Mary chose the good part, the "one thing," she wasn't rejecting forever all things domestic and earthly. There would always be meals to serve, beds to make, and dishes to wash. (Paraphrase of Jesus' words about the poor: "The projects you will always have with you."[9]) Her feet would remain firmly planted on terra firma. But by choosing the good part, she embraced the eternal.

Balance is impossible. Simplicity is important. Focus is imperative. Choosing is inevitable.

Now we're ready for "one thing."

TOO EASY TO BE TRUE?

The "one thing" isn't something we can get from a super-secret, high-powered, surefire list of steps in any book—including this one. It's not achieved by denying our natural Marthaness or faking an outward Maryness. It's not captured by working harder, longer, or even smarter.

"One thing" is not about being the right type.

"One thing" is not about following the right formula.

It's about love.

Just before Luke related our favorite story of Mary and Martha, he recounted Jesus' answer to the lawyer who asked which is the single most important commandment. His reply? "Love God. Love people." Read it for yourself below.

> "'Love the Lord your God with all your passion and prayer and intelligence.' This is the most important, the first on any list. But there is a second to set alongside it: 'Love others as well as you love yourself.'. . . Keep only these and you will find that you are obeying all the others."[10]

That just doesn't sound right, does it? It's too easy. Hmm. This calls for self-imposed complexity!

Remember the earlier comment of Paul about serving the Lord in simplicity? Here's the verse in its entirety: "But I am afraid that, as the serpent *deceived* Eve by his craftiness, your minds will be *led astray from the simplicity* and purity of devotion to Christ"[11] (italics added).

Notice the connection between deception and loss of simplicity? See how important it is for us to cling to truthful thinking? Faulty thought patterns blind us to simple truths. Believing lies keeps us in bondage to perfectionism and performance-based faith. Believing truth, including that only "one thing" is truly necessary, sets us free!

REINFORCEMENTS

Other New Testament verses affirm love as being the "one thing."[12]

"Walk in love."

"We ... ought to love one another."

"Be devoted to one another in brotherly love."

"You yourselves have been taught by God to love each other."

"Let us not love with words or tongue but with actions and in truth."

"The Lord make you to increase and abound in love to one another."

"Be completely humble and gentle; be patient, bearing with one another in love."

"Let all that you do be done with love."

"If I ... have not love, I am nothing."

"God is love."

Mary may have been helping Martha with meal preparations—to a point. Then perhaps she realized they had reached the level of "good enough"(simplifying). She intentionally reviewed her purpose (focusing). And, finally, she decided whether or not to be faithful to that purpose (choosing).

Love, the "one thing," is the paradigm by which we simplify, focus, and choose. When we find ourselves maxed out, a good question to ask ourselves is this: "Is *what* I'm doing, and the *way* I'm doing it, and the *why* I'm doing it showing love to God or to people?" If the answer is no, it's time to resimplify, refocus, and rechoose the good part. That will never be taken away from us.

EPILOGUE

We returned to the scene of the crime.

Ten years had passed since Teresa and I had set foot in the ministry where our Marthaness first went to the max—the same ministry where we had converted a jumbled and shabby store room into a "well-lighted showcase of our organizational ability."

Concluding our visit to a friend who still worked there, we decided to peek in the last room on the left.

Surprise, surprise.

If possible, it was even worse than its original condition when we worked there. The once-neat shelves sagged, barely visible beneath a hodgepodge of boxes, all of different sizes, many with water stains, few with lids, and none with labels. Empty fast-food wrappers scattered throughout added the smell of stale grease to that of dust and mildew. Yellow, orange, and brown electrical cords snaked among the debris littering the floor. We were sure, if we looked further, we'd find another bowling ball.

Teresa spoke first, but she said exactly what was on my mind.

"Aren't you glad we don't have to live like this anymore?"

Here's what she meant by that: We had no inclination to clean it ourselves, or to complain that someone else *ought to, needed to, or should.* We felt no anger, no frustration, and no guilt about this project that took so much and returned so little.

We were able to let it go.

We had been set free.

Through God's grace, *we* had been transformed inwardly into well-lighted showcases of Christ's redemptive ability. He took the stress, the deception, the workaholism, and even the perfectionism away.

You and Teresa and I may always have Martha qualities. There's nothing wrong with that. But taking them to the max is. The safeguard for us is simple.

May love always be first on our list.

CHAPTER EIGHTEEN

Resources

This part of the book is mostly a collection of things I've found useful, inspirational, or educational. Visit my Web site, too, for more exploration into all things Martha at www. maxedout.net

WHICH SIDE ARE WE ON?

For many of us Marthas, we're not dyed-in-the-wool perfectionists as much as we are pursuers of excellence. We may have even beat a path between the two so often that the Department of Transportation had to widen the road and put in a rest stop. The chart "The Fine Line Between," by Dr. David Stoop, a Christian psychologist, is one of the best I've seen to show the difference between excellence and perfectionism.

THE FINE LINE BETWEEN

Works for Me	*Works Against Me*
Excellence	Perfectionism
"Genuine striving"	Striving for "the ideal"
—personal best	

OUTLOOK
Realistic: "It is ..."	Idealistic: "It should be ..."

STRIVING FOR
The possible—	The impossible—
accepts the possible	desires the perfect

SELF-TALK
I want ...	I must ...
I wish ...	I should ...
I would like ...	I ought to ...

STATED AS
A request or desire	Always a demand

MOTIVATION
Striving for positive	Avoidance of negative
Desire for success	Fear of failure

FOCUS ON
Process	Product

EXPECTS
Best of self	Best in comparison to everyone else

LIFE VIEWED AS
Challenge that is welcomed	Curse that is dreaded

RESULTS
1. Accomplishment	1. Disappointment
2. Acceptance	2. Condemnation
3. Fulfillment	3. Frustration
4. Success	4. Failure

LIVE IN
Reality	Fantasy
Real world	Unreal world

BOTTOM LINE
THE TRUTH:	A LIE:
People and things do *not* have the ability to be perfect.	People and things have the ability to be perfect.

SOURCE: Dr. David Stoop, *Living with a Perfectionist* (Nashville: Oliver Nelson, 1987), 59. Used by permission of the publisher.

THE REAL YOU

As mentioned in chapter 8 ("The Worst Sin"), understanding and embracing our true identity in Christ is essential to happy and healthful living. Below is an excerpt from a list of affirmations for those who have accepted Jesus Christ as their Savior on an individual basis. These are worth reading and repeating on a daily basis.

The compiler of this list is Dr. Neil Anderson, founder of Freedom in Christ Ministries. He is the author of *The Bondage Breaker* (Harvest House) and *Victory over the Darkness* (Regal Books), in addition to speaking worldwide on the topic of freedom in Christ. You may order a "Who I Am in Christ" screen saver, audiocassette, or postcard from Freedom in Christ, 491 E. Lambert Road, La Habra, CA 90631; telephone 562-691-9128; fax 562-691-4035; Web site http://www.ficm.org. He offers a free, daily devotional by E-mail, too. Dr. Anderson urges, "The more you reaffirm who you are in Christ, the more your behavior will begin to reflect your true identity!"

Who I Am in Christ

I am accepted . . .

John 1:12	I am God's child.
Romans 5:1	I have been justified.
1 Corinthians 6:19–20	I have been bought with a price and I belong to God.
Ephesians 1:3–8	I have been chosen by God and adopted as His child.
Colossians 1:13–14	I have been redeemed and forgiven of all my sins.
Colossians 2:9–10	I am complete in Christ.
Hebrews 4:14–16	I have direct access to the throne of grace through Jesus Christ.

I am secure . . .

Romans 8:1–2	I am free from condemnation

Romans 8:28	I am assured that God works for my good in all circumstances.
Philippians 1:6	I am confident that God will complete the good work He started in me.
2 Timothy 1:7	I have not been given a spirit of fear but of power, love, and a sound mind.

I am significant . . .

John 15:5	I am a branch of Jesus Christ, the true vine, and a channel of His life.
John 15:16	I have been chosen and appointed to bear fruit.
Ephesians 2:6	I am seated with Jesus Christ in the heavenly realm.
Ephesians 3:12	I may approach God with freedom and confidence.
Philippians 4:13	I can do all things through Christ, who strengthens me.

NEAT FREAKS

Are you looking for ways to use your natural Martha skills? Here are some places to connect with others who also love to bring order out of chaos. (Some of them even get paid for it!)

National Association of Professional Organizers
P.O. Box 14067
Austin, TX 78714
Referral line: 512-206-0151
Fax: 512-454-3036
http://www.napo.net

HandyGirl Professional Organizing
9420 Reseda Blvd., Suite 234
Northridge, CA 91424
Telephone: 818-508-1555
Fax: 213-330-0221

E-mail: handygirl@organized-living.com
http://www.organized-living.com
Ask about Cyndi Seidler's book, *Organize for Success.*

International Association of Administrative Professionals
P.O. Box 20404
Kansas City, MO 64195-0404
Telephone: 816-891-6600
Fax: 816-891-9118
E-mail: service@iaap-hq.org
http://www.iaap-hq.org
Founded in 1942 as the National Secretaries Association, it went international in 1981 and now has 40,000 members in 700 chapters worldwide. IAAP offers professional development, networking opportunities, education, and a sample issue of its magazine.

NEAT FREAK WANNA-BES

Not all perfectionists live in immaculate homes or work in spotless offices. Perfectionism and procrastination are so closely related they're almost Siamese twins! A perfectionist might live in near-squalor, waiting until she has a perfect weekend free to clean her house. Until then, the laundry, dust, and dirty dishes pile up faster than the unread junk mail. If she has an office, she might postpone filing papers or recording data until she has time to create a perfect system (or is fired for misplacing crucial documents one time too many).

If you're a Martha held hostage by procrastination, here are some resources for you.

Don Aslett
c/o The Cleaning Center
P.O. Box 39
Pocatello, ID 83204
Telephone: 800-451-2402
Fax: 208-232-6286
http://www.cleanreport.com

Sandra Felton, founder of Messies Anonymous
5025 SW 114th Ave.
Miami, FL 33165
Telephone: 800-Mess-Away (800-637-7292)
Fax: 305-273-7671
http://www.messies.com
Sandra presents seminars, has a series of books for Messies, a newsletter, a video, a catalog of organizing tools, and support groups.

Barbara Hemphill, author of *Taming the Paper Tiger*
Hemphill & Associates, Inc.
1464 Garner Station Blvd. PMB 330
Raleigh, NC 27603
Telephone: 800-427-0237
Telephone: 919-773-0722
Fax: 919-773-0383
E-mail: barbara@hemphillandassociates.com
http://www.hemphillandassociates.com
http://www.thepapertiger.com
Both Web sites have abundant material to reduce time-wasting searches for paper and electronic documents, tips to sort papers just one time, and deal with mail quickly. Two credos on her site are "Asking for help is not a sign of weakness, but wisdom" and "Perfection prevents progress." If you want to be smart and move forward, check out Barbara's stuff.

Pat S. Moore, Queen of Clutter
10321 Doyle Blvd.
McKenney, VA 23872
Telephone: 804-478-5537
Fax: 804-478-5538
E-mail: patsmoore@aol.com
http://www.queenofclutter.com
Besides speaking to international audiences, Pat is a weekly columnist for *Women's World* on organization tips, offers the *Moore Clutter Control* newsletter, and is a frequent

guest expert on Home and Garden Television (HGTV). Her Web site has tips to help you save time and reduce clutter.

A DISORDER WITH TOO MUCH ORDER

Marthas, as we know, like to be in control of a clean and ordered environment. When this doesn't happen, we may not like it but we can live with it.

But there is another group of people for whom things like control, order, or cleanliness are not mere preferences. They are mandates—edicts from their own minds that are unassailable and nonnegotiable. This group of people suffers with *obsessive-compulsive disorder* (OCD). The "obsessive" part of the name comes from repetitive (and often unwanted or unpleasant) thoughts. "Compulsions" are behaviors to attempt to reduce the anxiety these obsessive thoughts bring.

OCD is frequently manifested by repetitious behavior, continual checking and rechecking (or cleaning and recleaning), extreme fear of contamination, or hoarding that can congest a house to the rafters with junk or odd collections.

OCD affects men and women equally and is found in every ethnic group, totaling about 2 percent of the world population. Patients with OCD have different patterns of brain activity from those without OCD. These patients also tend to respond well to medication to correct a deficiency in the brain chemical serotonin, suggesting that the problem is mostly neurological rather than the result of life or family experiences.[1]

Though the names are practically identical, the difference between OCD and *obsessive-compulsive personality* is substantial. The latter has a preoccupation with orderliness, perfectionism, and control but doesn't have obsessions or compulsions.[2]

Use your Internet search engine to locate the most current contact informatoin for OCD support groups and organizations.

Notes

Chapter 1: I Was Sinking Deep in Sin (Whee!)

1. Don Hawkins et al., *Before Burnout,* 2d ed. (Chicago: Moody, 1990), 184.
2. 1 John 3:2 NASB.
3. Proverbs 16:18 NASB.
4. Luke 10:41–42 NIV.

Chapter 2: Testing, Testing . . . How Much of a Martha Are You?

1. There is a wide difference between people with an obsessive personality and people with obsessive-compulsive disorder. OCD is a debilitating malady usually characterized by extreme rituals of cleaning and recleaning, checking and rechecking, or hoarding. OCD requires professional treatment. The obsessive personality is primarily characterized by perfectionism, which has twin needs of being in control and being perfect. Some of the traits related to perfectionism in the obsessive personality are "a fear of making errors; a fear of making a wrong decision or choice; a strong devotion to work; a need for order or firmly established routine; frugality; a need to know and follow the rules; emotional guardedness; a tendency to be stubborn or oppositional; a heightened sensitivity to being pressured or controlled by others; an inclina-

tion to worry, ruminate, or doubt; a need to be above criticism—moral, professional, or personal; cautiousness; a chronic inner pressure to use every minute productively." Allan E. Mallinger, M.D., and Jeanette DeWyze, *Too Perfect: When Being in Control Gets Out of Control* (New York: Clarkson Potter, 1992), 3.

Chapter 3: Martha's World: It Never Stops Spinning

1. *Merriam-Webster's Collegiate Dictionary,* 10th ed., s.vv. "Israel," "New Jersey"; John J. Pilch, *The Cultural Dictionary of the Bible* (Collegeville, Minn.: Liturgical, 1999), 40.
2. Pilch, *Cultural Dictionary of the Bible,* 178.
3. *Merriam-Webster's Collegiate Dictionary,* s.v. "Las Vegas"; Pilch, *Cultural Dictionary of the Bible,* 40.
4. http://www.jesus2000.com/other/bethany.htm.
5. http://comptonsv3.web.aol.com/s.../fastweb?getdoc+viewcomptons+AFP-SW+29151+6++Bethan.
6. John J. Bimson, *Baker Encyclopedia of Bible Places* (Grand Rapids: Baker, 1995), 66.
7. John J. Rousseau, *Jesus and His World* (Minneapolis: Augsburg Fortress, 1995), 16.
8. http://www.gnm.org/holyland/pilgrim118.htm.
9. M. G. Easton, *Easton's Bible Dictionary* (Oak Harbor, Wash.: Logos Research Systems, 1996). Electronic version.
10. Ibid.
11. Rousseau, *Jesus and His World,* 339.
12. Alfred Eidersheim, *The Life and Times of Jesus the Messiah,* Bible Explorer 2.0 (Epiphany Software, 1998).
13. *Enhanced Strong's Lexicon* (Oak Harbor, Wash.: Logos Research Systems, Inc., 1995).
14. *The Open Bible,* expand. ed. (Nashville: Thomas Nelson, 1983), 74.
15. *Nelson's Complete Book of Bible Maps and Charts* (Nashville: Thomas Nelson, 1996), 352.
16. http://www.jesus2000.com/other/bethany.htm.
17. Pilch, *Cultural Dictionary of the Bible,* 56, 57, 60, 180.
18. Rousseau, *Jesus and His World,* 16.
19. *Nelson's Complete Book of Bible Maps and Charts,* 169.
20. Ibid.
21. *The Open Bible,* 1,320–21.
22. Pilch, *Cultural Dictionary of the Bible,* 179.
23. Ibid., 89.
24. Rousseau, *Jesus and His World,* 339.
25. Pilch, *Cultural Dictionary of the Bible,* 88–89.
26. Rousseau, *Jesus and His World,* 339.
27. Ibid., 228-29.
28. Ibid., 128.
29. Ibid., 339.
30. Ibid.
31. Ibid., 129.
32. Ibid.

33. Fred H. Wight, *Manners and Customs of Bible Lands* (Chicago: Moody, 1952), 72.
34. Ibid., 62.
35. Ibid., 66.
36. Pilch, *Cultural Dictionary of the Bible,* 89.
37. Rousseau, *Jesus and His World,* 229.
38. Ibid., 129.
39. Ibid., 340.
40. Ibid., 339.
41. Eidersheim, *The Life and Times of Jesus,* 224.
42. Leland Ryken, James C. Wilhoit, and Tremper Longman III, eds., *Dictionary of Biblical Imagery* (Downers Grove, Ill.: InterVarsity, 1998), 403.
43. *Nelson's Complete Book of Bible Maps and Charts,* 319.
44. Eidersheim, *The Life and Times of Jesus,* 224.
45. Ibid.
46. Ibid., 225.
47. Ibid.
48. Ibid., 223.
49. Ryken, *Dictionary of Biblical Imagery,* 353
50. Ibid., 544; and Wight, *Manners and Customs of Bible Lands,* 83.
51. Charles W. Budden and Edward Hastings, *The Local Colour of the Bible* (Edinburgh: T. & T. Clark, 1925), 88–89.
52. Ryken, *Dictionary of Biblical Imagery,* 544.
53. Pilch, *Cultural Dictionary of the Bible,* 58; and Wight, *Manners and Customs of Bible Lands,* 43.
54. Pilch, *Cultural Dictionary of the Bible,* 58.
55. Ryken, *Dictionary of Biblical Imagery,* 402.
56. Ibid., 403.
57. Deuteronomy 10:19.
58. Matthew 25:35 NIV; Matthew 10:5–15.
59. Ryken, *Dictionary of Biblical Imagery,* 403.
60. Ibid., 403.
61. Budden and Hastings, *Local Colour of the Bible,* 90–92.
62. Ryken, *Dictionary of Biblical Imagery,* 403.
63. Ibid.
64. Pilch, *Cultural Dictionary of the Bible,* 36.
65. Ibid., 37.
66. Genesis 18:1–15; 1 Samuel 25:14–42; 1 Kings 17:8–16.
67. Ryken, *Dictionary of Biblical Imagery,* 960.
68. Ibid., 961.
69. Pilch, *Cultural Dictionary of the Bible,* 5.

Chapter 4: The Strife of the Party

1. James Hastings, *The Greater Men and Women of the Bible* (New York: Scribners, 1915), 321.
2. Jesus' cleansing of the temple, John 2:13–16 in A.D. 27; Galilean miracles, John 4:46–54; Luke 4:31–5:26; Matthew 14:22–33; Jerusalem healings, John 5:1–17 in A.D. 28 and John 9:1–41 in A.D. 29; disciples selected, Luke 6:12–16 in A.D. 28; women companions, Matthew 27:55–56; Mark 15:40–41; Luke

8:1–3; possible maximum group size, Keith Miller, professor of New Testament studies at Calvary Bible College in Kansas City, Missouri; telephone interview, 3 February 2000.

3. W. E. Vine, Merrill F. Unger, and William White, *Vine's Complete Expository Dictionary of Old and New Testament Words* [computer file], electronic ed., Logos Library System (Nashville: Thomas Nelson, 1997, © 1996).

4. John J. Pilch, *The Cultural Dictionary of the Bible* (Collegeville, Minn.: Liturgical, 1999), 46–47, 60.

5. James M. Freeman, *Hand-Book of Bible Manners and Customs* (Cincinnati: Cranston & Stowe, 1874), 424. See also Leland Ryken, James C. Wilhoit, and Tremper Longman III, eds., *Dictionary of Biblical Imagery* (Downers Grove, Ill.: InterVarsity, 1998), 961.

6. Vine, Unger, and White, *Vine's Complete Expository Dictionary of Old and New Testament Words* [computer file].

7. Storm, Mark 4:38; hired hand, John 10:13; Judas, John 12:6.

8. Luke 22:31; Matthew 23:37; Acts 9:4; Luke 10:41.

9. "The repetition of her name conveys a mild rebuke or lament," *The New Interpreter's Bible* (Nashville: Abingdon, 1995), 232. "The repetition of the name is gently critical," John Nolland, *Luke 9:21–18:34,* vol. 35B, *Word Biblical Commentary* (Dallas: Word, 1993), 605.

10. John 11:5.

11. *Agapaō* (ἀγαπάω) applied to persons means "to welcome, to entertain, to be fond of, to love dearly." *Enhanced Strong's Lexicon,* electronic ed. (Oak Harbor, Wash.: Logos Research Systems, 1995).

12. Vine, Unger, and White, *Vine's Complete Expository Dictionary of Old and New Testament Words* [computer file].

13. *Merriam-Webster's Collegiate Dictionary,* 10th ed., s.v. "turbulent."

Chapter 5: It's Not Just Me: Meet My Martha Buddies

1. Jason A. McGarvey, quoting Robert B. Slaney in "The Almost Perfect Definition," *Research* (Pennsylvania State Univ.) 17 (September 1996). Http://www.research.psu.edu/rps/sep96/almost.html.

Chapter 6: The Martha of the New Millennium

1. Ellen Sue Stern, *The Indispensable Woman* (New York: Bantam, 1988), 21.

2. Joseph S. Carroll, *How to Worship Jesus Christ* (reprint; Chicago: Moody, 1991), 27.

3. Ibid., 26.

4. Second Corinthians 4:18 NIV.

5. Psalm 39:4–6.

Chapter 7: Personality Type or Hype?

1. http://www.axiomsoftware.com/history.html.

2. Ibid.

3. http://www.aptcentral.org/aptmbtiw.htm.

4. Martin and Deidre Bobgan, *Four Temperaments, Astrology and Personality Testing* (Santa Barbara: PsychoHeresy Awareness Ministries, 1992). http://www.psychoheresy-aware.org.

5. John Trent and Gary Smalley, *The Treasure Tree* (Dallas: Word Kids, 1992).
6. John M. Oldham, M.D., and Lois B. Morris, *Personality Self-Portrait: Why You Think, Work, Love, and Act the Way You Do* (New York: Bantam, 1990), 396.
7. Ibid.
8. Richard A. Swenson, M.D., *The Overload Syndrome: Learning to Live Within Your Limits* (Colorado Springs: NavPress, 1998), 31–33.
9. Ibid., 32.
10. Ibid., 33.
11. 1 Peter 3:7 NIV.
12. Genesis 1:1 NIV; Hebrews 11:3 NIV; Revelation 4:11 NIV.
13. Deuteronomy 10:17 NIV; Acts 10:34 NIV; Romans 2:11 NIV; 2 Peter 3:9 NIV.
14. Cain and Abel, Genesis 4; Ishmael and Isaac, Genesis 16 and 21; Jacob and Esau, Genesis 25:21–34; 33:1–20; Joseph, Genesis 37; Leah and Rachel, Genesis 28–30.
15. Acts 15:36–40.
16. 2 Chronicles 2.
17. Matthew 16:18 NIV; 1 Corinthians 12:27 NIV.
18. Romans 12 and 14 NIV; 2 Corinthians 10:12–13, 17 NIV; Galatians 6:3 NIV.
19. Romans 14:19 NIV.
20. Ephesians 4:31–32 NIV; 1 Peter 4:8 NIV; 1 Corinthians 6:19–20 NIV, 1 Peter 3:2–10 NASB.

Chapter 8: The Worst Sin

1. Stars, Psalm 147:4 NIV; angels, Hebrews 12:22 NIV; Gabriel, Luke 1:11–22, 26–38; Michael, Jude 9 and Revelation 12:7–9.
2. Ezekiel 28:13, followed by Isaiah 14:11, both texts from the NIV.
3. Isaiah 14:14 NIV.
4. David Stoop, M.D., *Living with a Perfectionist* (Kansas City: Nelson, 1987), 52.
5. 2 Corinthians 11:14.
6. 1 John 4:4 NASB.
7. John 8:44.
8. John 8:31–32 NIV.
9. "Accuser," Revelation 12:10.
10. "The angel of the Abyss, whose name in Hebrew is *Abaddon,* and in Greek, *Apollyon,*" (Revelation 9:11 NIV italics added) . Both terms mean "destroyer." M. G. Easton, *Easton's Bible Dictionary* (Oak Harbor, Wash.: Logos Research Systems, 1996.

Chapter 9: Keeping Up Appearances

1. Miriam Elliott and Susan Meltsner, *The Perfectionist Predicament: How to Stop Driving Yourself and Others Crazy* (New York: William Morrow, 1991), 30–31.
2. Ibid.
3. Adam and Eve, Genesis 3:8; Ananias and Sapphira, Acts 5:1–11; Jesus and the Pharisees, Matthew 23:27.

Chapter 10: Anger, Fear, and Guilt: Are We Having Fun Yet?

1. David Seamands, *Freedom from the Performance Trap* (Wheaton, Ill.: Victor, 1988), 168. Italics are Seamands's.

2. http://www.christianityonline.com/tcw/2000/001/1.22.html.
3. Ephesians 2:3; Galatians 5:20.
4. Allan E. Mallinger, M.D., and Jeanette DeWyze, *Too Perfect: When Being in Control Gets Out of Control* (New York: Clarkson Potter, 1992), 14.
5. Bill Hybels, *Who You Are When No One's Looking* (Downers Grove, IL: Inter-Varsity, 1987), 104–5.
6. Leviticus 22:19–24.
7. Jean Fleming, *Finding Focus in a Whirlwind World* (Fort Collins, Colo.: Treasure! 1991), 13–14.
8. Peg Rankin, *How to Care for the Whole World and Still Take Care of Yourself* (Nashville: Broadman & Holman, 1994), ix–x.

Chapter 11: Martha Moms: The Perils of Perfectionistic Parenting

1. Susan L. Lenzkes, "Parenthood," copyright 1981. Used by permission.
2. In an informal survey, kids described how they would change their parents: "I would ask them to love me." "I tell them to love me." "I would have them love me more." "I would ask them to love me more." "I would want them to . . . show love instead of anger or impatience." "Let them be loving parents." "I would ask them to love me in every thing I do." "I would teach them to hug me and tell me they love me . . . I only wish they would hug me." The authors conclude, "A child must be assured that his parents accept him independently of his performance." Bill Orr and Erwin Lutzer, *If I Could Change My Mom and Dad* . . . (Chicago: Moody, 1983), 18–27, 137.
3. Dr. Chuck Lynch, *Perfectionism: How to Gain Release from the Performance Trap,* audiocassette (Blue Springs, Mo.: Living Foundation Ministries, 1993).
4. Lynch, telephone interview, 4 January 2000.

Chapter 12: Post-Project Depression (Stretch Marks Not Included)

1. http://infotrail.com/dad/html/feelings.html.
2. 1 Kings 18–19.
3. First and last, Matthew 20:16; wise and foolish, 1 Corinthians 3:18; strength and weakness, 2 Corinthians 12:10.
4. Dale Ryan and Juanita Ryan, "Asking for Support," electronic document from Christian Recovery International. Http://www.christianrecovery.com/askhelp.htm.
5. Joni Eareckson Tada, quoted in Joseph Stowell, *Far from Home* (Chicago: Moody, 1998), 130.
6. 2 Corinthians 12:9, *The Message.*
7. Roxie Ann Wessels, Telephone interview and fax transmission, 10 February 2000.
8. Richard Swenson, M.D., *The Overload Syndrome* (Colorado Springs: NavPress, 1998), 77.
9. John 8:32 NIV.
10. Neil Anderson, *Daily in Christ* (Eugene, Oreg.: Harvest House, 1993), reading for November 1.

Chapter 13: Holidays, Schmolidays (Or, Six Hours One Wednesday)

1. Frank Minirth, Don Hawkins, and Paul Meier, *Happy Holidays* (Grand Rapids: Baker, 1990), 58–59.

Chapter 14: Hurry Up and Relax!

1. Deuteronomy 5: 6–21.
2. Numbers 15:32–41.
3. Christine M. Bryla, "The Relationship Between Stress and the Development of Breast Cancer: A Literature Review," *Oncology Nursing Forum* 23 (January/February 1996): 442.
4. Ibid.
5. Ibid., 441.
6. "Cortisol is a hormone released by the adrenal cortex during the 'fight or flight' stress response. It causes gluconeogenesis, the breakdown of fats and proteins for fuel. Breakdown of fat is usually not harmful, but prolonged breakdown of proteins for fuel can increase susceptibility to cancer (Allen, 1983). Protein is the main ingredient in white blood cells. When cortisol causes the breakdown of protein for energy, as during the stress response, it leaves the immune system with insufficient raw material to create and mature new cells. Ultimately, this suppresses the monitoring effectiveness of the immune system. The chances of malignant cells going unchecked and establishing a tumor are thereby increased (Allen, 1983)." Bryla, *Oncology Nursing Forum*, 445.

Chapter 15: Work Now, Sleep Never

1. John Shepard Jr., M.D., telephone interview, 27 January 2000.
2. Sleep Disorders Unit, Epworth Hospital, Melbourne, Australia; http://www.drkoop.com/tools/calculator/sleep.asp.
3. http://sleepmed.bsd.uchicago.edu/circadianrhythms.html.
4. http://www.sfn.org/briefings/bio_clocks.html.
5. "Perfect love casts out fear, because fear involves torment" (1 John 4:18). *The Living Bible* says it well, too: "We need have no fear of someone who loves us perfectly; his perfect love for us eliminates all dread of what he might do to us. If we are afraid, it is for fear of what he might do to us, and shows that we are not fully convinced that he really loves us."
6. "Then you will know the truth, and the truth will set you free" (John 8:32 NIV).
7. Richard A. Swenson, M.D., *Margin: Restoring Emotional, Physical, Financial, and Time Reserves to Overloaded Lives* (Colorado Springs: NavPress, 1992), 129.

Chapter 16: Buckle Up! We Are Now Entering Reality

1. Cheryl Gochnauer, telephone interview, 10 January 2000.
2. Barbara Hemphill, author of *Taming the Paper Tiger*. Quote taken from the Web site http://www.thepapertiger.com or http://www.hemphillandassociates.com.
3. Jean Fleming, *Finding Focus in a Whirlwind World* (Fort Collins, Colo.: Treasure! 1991), 63.
4. 1 John 4:6 NIV.
5. 1 John 4:16 NIV.
6. Psalms 86:5; 103:8; Daniel 9:18 NIV; Luke 6:36 NIV.
7. Deuteronomy 7:6–9; John 1:17; 2 Corinthians 12:9 NIV.
8. Isaiah 9:6; 26:3; 54:10; Psalm 29:11; John 14:27.

Chapter 17: One (More) Thing

1. http://www.aphorismsgalore.com/author/Karl_Wallenda.html.
2. 2 Corinthians 11:3 NASB.
3. Jean Fleming, *Finding Focus in a Whirlwind World* (Fort Collins, Colo.: Treasure! 1991), 60.
4. Richard Warren, *The Purpose-Driven Church* (Grand Rapids: Zondervan, 1995).
5. Romans 12; 1 Corinthians 12; Ephesians 4; 1 Peter 4.
6. Willow Creek Resources, *Network: The Right People in the Right Places for the Right Reasons* at http://www.willowcreek.org/Resources/RSCNetwork. html; or Willow Creek Community Church, 67 East Algonquin Road, South Barrington, IL 60010 (847-765-5000).
7. Fleming, *Finding Focus in a Whirlwind World*, 40.
8. Luke 6:12–16; W. E. Vine, Merrill F. Unger, and William White, *Vine's Complete Expository Dictionary of Old and New Testament Words* [computer file], electronic ed., Logos Library System (Nashville: Thomas Nelson, 1997, © 1996).
9. Matthew 26:11.
10. Matthew 22:37–39 *The Message*; Matthew 22:40 TLB.
11. 2 Corinthians 11:3 NASB.
12. The list comes from Ephesians 5:2; 1 John 4:11 NIV; Romans 12:10 NIV; 1 Thessalonians 4:9 NIV; 1 John 3:18 NIV; 1 Thessalonians 3:12; Ephesians 4:2 NIV; 1 Corinthians 16:14; 1 Corinthians 13:2 NIV; 1 John 4:8 NIV.

Chapter 18: Resources

1. R. L. DuPont, D. P. Rice, S. Shiraki, and C. Rowland, *Economic costs of obsessive-compulsive disorder.* Unpublished, 1994. Referenced from the OCD Web site of the National Institute of Health at http://www.nimh.nih.gov/publicat/ ocd.htm.
2. American Psychiatric Association, *Diagnostic and Statistical Manual of Mental Disorders,* 4th ed., 1994.